Chapman 84

George Mackay Brown: an a...

Illustrations:
Alfons Bytautas, Emilio Coia, Trish
Edwards, Jules George, Mary Gibons,
Stephen Lee and "Spike"
Special thanks to Archie Bevan

ISBN 0 906772 76 1   ISSN 0308-2695   © *Chapman* 1996

CHAPMAN

4 Broughton Place, Edinburgh EH1 3RX, Scotland
Tel 0131 557 2207 Fax 0131–556 9565
Editor: Joy Hendry   **Associate Editor: Robert Calder**
Editorial Assistant: Sam Wood
Volunteers:
Katie Lockwood, Alan Pattullo, Louise Robb, Jerry Stewart &Tara Wynn

Submissions:
Chapman welcomes submissions of poetry,
fiction and critical articles provided they are
accompanied by a stamped addressed envelope
or International Reply coupons

Subscriptions:

	Personal		Institutional	
	1 year	2 years	1 year	2 years
UK	£14	£26	£19	£35
Overseas	£19/$32	£35/$59	£23/$39	£42/$69

THE SCOTTISH ARTS COUNCIL

THE CITY OF EDINBURGH DISTRICT COUNCIL
EDINBURGH
IMPROVING SERVICES – CREATING JOBS

Printed by The Cromwell Press Ltd, Broughton Gifford, Melksham, Wiltshire, SN12 8PH.

Illustration by Alfons Bytautas

The Man on the Shore

George Mackay Brown

There was once an island in the north, between two oceans.

A fisherman kept his boat on the beach and between storms he would sail out and catch a few haddocks or crabs for his wife and children.

There was a hill between him and a small croft. There, a year before, a man had dug and drained the earth, and made a few furrows with an ox and sowed seed, and cut an oat harvest at the end of summer. There was enough bread to see him and his wife and young children through the first winter. The following year, he had enough coins put by to buy a cow and a dozen sheep.

They knew they were not alone in the place. Sometimes they glimpsed a man on the shore, going like the shadow of a cloud. An otter trotted beside the man with a fish in its mouth.

Sometimes the fisherman and the crofter would see each other in the distance, and a cry of greeting flew from one to the other.

They had been seamen on a galley out of Norway, seeking land in the west. The skipper and the young adventurers had taken over the most fertile islands. Those two oarsmen, of small consequence, were given a little barren island to settle in.

The crofter came closer one day. He asked if he could get stones from the shore to build a byre, a winter shelter, for his cow.

"Take what you want," said the fisherman. "There are thousands of stones."

Another time, the fisherman asked if he could cut some heather from the hill to weave into lobster creels. "Help yourself," said the crofter.

After more than a year in that lonely island, the crofter and the fisherman sometimes exchanged produce: a string of haddocks for a small white cheese.

There was no boundary between their domains. Still, whenever they met for a few words, they seemed to know where to meet each other – on the rock at the foot of the hill, or on either side of the burn that ran and chattered down to the sea.

The wives rarely spoke to each other.

But the three children of the fisherman and the two children of the crofter ran together across the hill with kites whenever the wind blew in spring.

As the years passed, the fisherman and the crofter were aware that other people were coming in to live in their poor island.

A ship-load of new immigrants had arrived from the fjords. Families were set down on this island and that. A man with two pairs of horses and four tall sons and daughters and a domineering wife had established a farm on the far side of the island. They built a fence all round it.

Soon there was a third farmer, and a fourth and a fifth farmer. It seemed the soil of the island was richer than anyone had known up to then.

And the fisherman, walking round the island shore one day, saw black tarred wooden bothies on this sheltered noust and that, and strangers working to make new boats ready for the spring fishing.

"There's not enough fish in the sea for so many boats," he called to the strangers, one after the other, but they turned stone faces on him.

As for the incoming women, they curled their lips at him, silently. That such a poor man should try to give advice to their adventurous men-folk!

And the strange-voiced children threw stones at him!

"It looks as if there might be hungrier times in this island," the fisherman said to his wife. "Too many yoles and lines, too few fish."

"There's plenty for everybody and spare," said the wife, rocking a new cradle.

That summer, in the dry month of June, the new crofters and the new fishermen ran out of water from their rain barrels, and then they came to ask the crofter and the fisherman if they might use the well beside the rock – a bucket or two till the rain came.

The original islanders consulted each other beside the shrunken burn. They agreed that it would be too bad if the new families, especially the children, suffered because of the drought. "There's plenty of rain out there," they said, pointing out to the Atlantic Ocean. "Let them have a few bucketfuls till the rain comes. The water's not ours, anyway."

"You're fools," said the crofter's wife. "You should have charged them a penny a bucket. There's not all that much water in the well. They can afford a penny a bucket. They have bigger fields and more cows and sheep than we have. And your friend, Frakok the fisherman, his boat's a miserable-looking thing compared to their new yoles. His net is mostly rags. And his wife's a gormless slut."

Still the drought lasted. The islands women gathered twice a day at the well with their buckets, and they got to know each other and exchanged news. Even the fisherman's wife and the crofter's wife joined that chorus of women, morning and evening, and they seemed to enjoy the splurges of gossip and speculation. Just occasionally, if they filled their buckets so full that water overbrimmed and splashed on the stones, the croft wife would look stern and say, in the middle of some idle story, "Go careful, the well's almost dry! It hasn't rained now for six weeks. And you're not paying for your water any more."

Then the women would take up their buckets and go silently homeward, each along her own track.

One morning in mid-July the islanders woke to the surge of rain on their roofs. They could not see the top of the hill Fea for a cloud. The sea was dull as pewter. The rain streamed and surged. The water barrels brimmed and brimmed.

The forty children of the island ran out into the downpour, laughing and singing. They made cups of their hands. They threw water at each other.

The new islanders, who were much cleverer and more progressive than the first fisherman and the first crofter, sounded out three new water-sources with twigs, and dug wells there.

They began, once more, to think poorly of those poor men and their poor families.

None of them trusted the man who wandered about the tide-line, putting shells and crabs into a bag, the otter at his heels like a shadow.

They fenced and dug and drained and ploughed and sowed. They probed new fishing grounds westward. They were not always successful. But the first fisherman rarely returned without a few fish or crabs.

And the first crofter and his family always had something to eat, a bowl of porridge or an oatcake, with butter and cheese; for now they had a cow, a goat, and six sheep, a meagre stock compared to the new farms all around his six unfenced acres: they managed to get through the winter, he and his growing children, but at the end of one winter there were thin blue hands on the young ones.

"You should go and ask Ragnar and Sigurd for a few pieces of smoked meat," said Bui the crofter's wife. "They have plenty hanging from their rafters. After all, we let them have water for nothing, the summer before last, in the big drought."

But the crofter was as stubborn as his ox. He would rather die than beg for food!

One morning Ingi the crofter's wife opened her door and found six haddocks on the doorstep.

"It's Hild the fisherman's wife," said Bui the crofter. "I wish you would speak more kindly to her."

"Hild wouldn't part with a haddock's eye."

"It's an angel from heaven left it at the door," said Ingi. "I said a prayer last night, and look, it's been answered."

The fisherman went out that same morning to open his door. There was a clutch of gulls' eggs on the doorstep.

"Bui has been to the crag for eggs," he said to his wife.

"Never ask where the eggs came from. Put them in the pot, man. Blow up the fire. Bui's terrified of crags. It wasn't him or his trollop that left them on our doorstep."

Then she crossed herself.

ii

A thousand years have passed.

It is the same island. There are bigger farms, with oat-fields and barley-fields from the uplands to the shore, and horses, cows, sheep and alert dogs. There is a village down at the shore, where the burn empties into the sea. There is an inn, a kirk, a smithy, a general merchant's store, and a dozen houses. In the heart of the island, surrounded by trees, is the big house, the laird's, who is sometimes in the island but always, in winter especially, in his Edinburgh house.

It is quiet in the island, because it is Sunday. But soon families begin to emerge from the farms and crofts and troop solemnly towards the kirk.

It is Harvest Thanksgiving Day. The harvest is late this year, because the summer was wet and cold; and only a few fields have been cut, but the standing corn promises well. Given a good September, with sun and wind, the harvest will be good, and well worth giving thanks for.

Now the people are in their pews in the kirk. Their little kirk is transfigured! The produce of the year – the very best – is stacked here and there about the choir and against the pulpit steps: turnips and cabbages big as cannon-balls, sheaves of oats that let fall a golden whisper now and then, round white cheeses, baskets of eggs, a white fleece and a black fleece, mounds of potatoes, plates with blond cubes of butter on them.

The kirk is like a little ark well stored for the voyage into winter.

The fifteen families are well pleased. They have brought all this benison to the kirk themselves. The women have spent a long day arranging the produce and setting jars of flowers here and there in the kirk windows.

It has been well done.

The minister has ascended into the pulpit and the beadle is just about to close the kirk door when a man and his wife and three young children arrive, with the breath on their lips.

Everybody knows this family, the Bews of Biggings, the poorest and most backward country-folk in the island. James Bews still farms the way his great-grandfather did a hundred years earlier, with two oxen and a wooden plough. He has lately been in trouble for not sending his children to the island school, in contravention of the Education Act of 1872. "I needed them to work in the tattie-field," had been his excuse to the magistrate, who had let him off with a warning; "but next time, my man, you'll get a hefty fine, mark my words."

"You're late," said the beadle: "Can't you hear, they're singing the opening psalm . . . What's this?"

Kitty Bews was offering a straw basket covered with a cloth. "For the thanksgiving," said Kitty.

"Too late," said the beadle. "All contributions should have been in yesterday afternoon. Just leave it here. Go in and be quiet."

The Bews family of Biggings crept into their pew as quiet as mice.

The beadle took the covering off the basket. There were five oatcakes in it – they had the warmth of sun and griddle in them still.

The psalm was over. The congregation was sitting to hear the reading from the Old Testament. Even if the congregation was otherwise unaware of the presence of the Bews family, a smell would have told them: an earth smell, a smell of peat fires and roots.

The folk of Biggings were clean and decently turned out, but these ancient earthy smells went with them always, and was specially noticeable on Sundays, in the cold clean air of the kirk.

A widow in the Old Testament was making a small cake for the prophet with the last of her meal and oil . . .

The congregation heard another slight disturbance at the entrance to the kirk. The beadle, grumbling, was having to open the door to other latecomers . . .

"Late again!" whispered the beadle harshly to Jock Voes and his trauchled wife and five bairns. "Do you think the service is always going to wait for you? Have some respect. What's in this sack? Leave it, leave it. You can't take it into the kirk, it's oozing sea-water. Go on, get in. No point going in once the sermon starts, you'd been better biding home."

The beadle untied the sack. In it were a lobster and a crab, scrabbling. Jock Voes was a fisherman.

(The historian who had lately visited the island had announced to the astonishment of everyone that this poorest man in the island was a direct descendant of the first Norwegian settler.)

The laird had been very intrigued when the historian had read his paper at the Antiquarian Society in Kirkwall. He had called in at the Voes' house above the shore and laid a sovereign on the table. "Voes," he said, "it ought to be you by rights who's sitting in the big carved chair up at The Hall, not me!"

Be that as it may, the Voes were the very poorest folk in the island . . . Several of the crofters went fishing when the weather was promising, to eke out their living. Of recent years they had begun to put engines in their yoles, and so were not slaves to a contrary wind. But Jock Voes stuck to his patched boat, and his patched sail took him to his ancestral fishing grounds, often quite far out, under the horizon; and on good days he seemed to have heavier catches than the 'progressive' fishermen. But there were weeks on end, when the wind sat snarling and raging in the east, when all he could do was rifle the rockpools for limpets, and mend old creels, and gather driftwood.

Then Annie Voes ran up debts in the general merchants.

The congregation, half way through the hymn, 'Eternal Father, strong to save', was aware of a heavy incense of salt and fishiness. They looked askance from their hymn-books. It was – they knew it – Jock Voes and his family, come late as usual.

The precentor turned and sat down. The congregation sat down. The Voes family sat down. The minister, the Rev Thomas McGillivray, read that part of the scripture that deals with the feeding of the multitude with five barley loaves and two fishes.

The laird arrived late, just as the sermon began. He was shown into his pew in the gallery by Garson the beadle. The laird only attended the kirk this one Sabbath of the year, Harvest Thanksgiving: he was an Episcopalian like all the lairds, and attended the chanted services in Kirkwall. But he always turned up with his five sovereigns to put in the plate on Harvest Thanksgiving Sunday . . .

Just as the long sermon was ending, to everyone's relief, for Rev Thomas McGillivray's sermons were like the thunder of millstones that yielded a poke of meal at best, there was a cry outside. Billyon the beachcomber was standing among the tombstones.

He always got a few turnips and cabbages after Harvest Thanksgiving.

"Don't make such an outcry," said the beadle.

Billyon stood there as if he had all the patience in the world. He stood there as if the little kirk, sailing with its cargo of earth fruit, belonged as much to him, the man of hunger, as to the laird, the farmers, and the fishing folk.

iii

A hunger fell on all the earth.

At first, slowly, people began to wither before their time.

The islanders looked at each other, bewildered and ashamed and angry. They had been brought up to believe that 'the standard of living' would improve, each generation better off than their fathers. And so it had seemed, for seven or eight generations.

There was a prospect of boundless freedom, a kind of earthly paradise. The restraints of religion were thrown aside, like shackles.

Education, science, technology, were beginning to flood the earth with a new 'power and glory'. The whole of creation was there to be exploited.

People lived much longer for two centuries, but their lives had little meaning, other than newspaper oracles, or the promised miracles of science. Small womb-cloistered children were killed before they had time to breathe the air, drink from a burn, feel the sun on their hands among the grass.

Then the slow poisoning began. The earth and the sea were polluted. The legions of fish round the coasts thinned to a few sickly loiterers.

The women on the farms bought their bread from cities in the south, and the bread was light and tasteless.

The air began to be polluted.

In the island more and more children were maimed with asthma and bronchial afflictions. The 'petrol-drinkers', cars and tractors, were blamed, but still in the year 2000 AD every house had its car, and sometimes two or three. The car was the sign and the seal of the heaven-on-earth to come.

They were uneasy at the nuclear reactor a few miles from them, and the proposed importation of spent uranium for burial from all the great nations on earth. But they had still unbounded faith in the infallible priesthood of science; those magi knew how to contain risks and dangers, surely.

The blow-out of a Russian nuclear reactor made our islanders pause and think for a few minutes, now and again. But the poison clouds blowing about in the atmosphere seemed to be affecting only reindeer herds in Lapland and (strangely) flocks of sheep in Wales.

There certainly seemed to be more cancers than formerly.

Crime burgeoned everywhere, as if some moral stems and buds in humanity had never been given a chance to develop.

Most appalling of all, some of the innocent peoples of the world, the 'noble savages', having been given the benefit of our education and religion and democratic systems of government, turned on each other with appalling savagery, tribe against tribe, with the guns we had sold them and entrusted to their natural self-control and pure judgement.

All this the people in our island saw, night after night, on their television screens. And they saw, too, a green growing scum on the waters around them, the lochs and the oceans.

The very old men declared that the level of the sea was rising. Rocks at

high tide were covered that had stood there unwashed since their childhood. Year after year, a great battlement of cliff collapsed into the sea.

Did it matter if a thousand trees an hour were felled in a great rain forest
on the far side of the earth? What was it to them, the livelihood of a few
naked tribes, along the upper Amazon?

People hungered for something beyond their shuttered selves, as they
had done from the beginning: a desire to be part of the dance of the seasons and the stars in their courses – not to 'understand' the mysteries of
time and being, only to rejoice in dawn and sunset, spring and harvest,
alpha and omega. But ceremony was only, now, a lingering branch of
ancient superstition, that withered in the new age, and rightly so . . . There
were distillations and essences of flowers and roots that seemed, fleetingly,
to bring the longed-for nirvana close: the drug culture of the young.

Slates fell in a torrent from the kirk one winter storm and were not
replaced, because they no longer had a minister, only one who called once
a month from another island.

The psalms of David were going down, all over the world, before the
money-fuelled ecstasies of American revivalists; but not in this island,
where the people have always spoken as few words as were needed, and
thought it shame to show their emotions in public.

They did believe, whole-heartedly, for six or seven generations, on the
nirvana of progress to which they had pledged themselves.

Time was linear, not any more a cycle – "a time to sow and a time to reap,
a time to mourn and a time to dance . . ."

Money, profit, was the life-blood of this new religion . . . With the erod-
ing of the ten laws hewn on the Sinai stone, one need not be too particular
how one took one's share. The prisons became colleges of crime, as the
thieves and villains put their heads together.

The island people shook their heads. All this crime was happening far
away, in the cities. One or two of the islanders noticed that their own young
people were being touched by the taint, too, increasingly. Instead of being
ashamed at having to appear in the Sheriff Court – as they would have been
in their own youth – the "teenagers" boasted about; it was a sign of their
manhood; they had come through the initiation rites into the new time.

Then, quite suddenly – in the space of a decade – there were no fish in
the sea. The big fishing boats – far bigger than the little yoles of their fathers
– lay warping and rusting at the piers because the sea had been overfished
by increasingly efficient fleets.

The good earth lost its fertility, over a longer period, a generation.

Life in the islands was meaningless at first, then dangerous as the green
grass struggled out of the earth gray and moulded. (They had long ceased
to grow oats and barley). Cows and sheep got diseases unknown before.

The people left the island for the cities, where the money was, like
starved bees smelling nectar in distant orchards. All the people left all the
islands: individually, by families, by entire communities.

One old man drifted along the shore, but even the driftwood had given
out.

There were no more fish boxes, no more barrel staves; only dead fish that glowed like dying lanterns and then went out.

The old man sat on the rock with a black otter at his feet, and chewed his cut of tobacco, and spat.

*

A thousand years have passed.

Twelve young monks came to the island in a boat made of ox-hides stretched over a wooden frame.

"A blessing on you, good island in the sea," said Brendan the abbot who navigated the boat.

The island made no reply.

"This island is as dead as all the others," said Brother Malachi.

"This is an island on the way," said Brendan. "We will go ashore here. We must live here for a while, I think."

Not a bird spoke to them on the shore.

"How can we live in this wilderness in the sea?" said Brother Finn.

"There is a good enough cave," said Brendan the abbot. "We'll be sheltered there in winter."

"But there's nothing to eat," said Liam the youngest monk. "The sea is empty. There are not even berries among the heather. Not a tree for kindling."

"We'll go ashore now."

They dropped into the sea one after the other, and walked with sodden robes towards the shore of the dead island. Their hands and feet and throats shone.

"We'll stop in this fine inn," said Brendan, pointing to the cave. "We'll get a good welcome, I think."

There was a fire of driftwood and peats burning in the cave. The brothers stood round the fire until they were dry.

An old man came into the cave and added more peats to the fire and went out again.

"Who was that old man?" said Brother Maurice.

"He's the angel who looks after the island," said Brendan.

The old man came back with a plate and a jug. There were pieces of bread on the plate and water in the pot.

"Have your supper," said the old man. "Your coats are dry now. There's nothing here for you. You're just a nuisance as far as I'm concerned. Beds? Sleep on the stones. Be off the island at first light . . ."

Then he went away, and an otter trotted at his heels.

"What an awkward creature," said Brother Brian.

They said a blessing over the food and ate the first meal on shore since sailing from home. The old man came in with a candle that he set in a niche. He was grumbling and growling still in his beard. He took away the jug and the plate.

"We are honoured to be ministered to by an angel," said Brendan. "This is the courtesy of heaven."

They sang compline as the first star looked in at the cave mouth. They slept till the sun got up. Then they said matins.

"I suppose you'll be wanting a bite of breakfast before you sail off," said the old man. "I have more to do than look after a gang of sea tramps like you. I'm old and tired and full of rheumatics."

"Count yourselves blessed," said Brendan to the brothers, "that you've heard the speech of an angel, even in the time of this mortal life . . . Before we gorge ourselves on this breakfast, we'll say Mass."

"But, Brendan," said Brother Donal, "we have no wine for the offering."

But, when Brendan looked into the deep clay chalice, the brothers saw how his sea-gray face flushed with the travail and joy of wine presses. And so they could offer Mass in the island.

"Now," said Brendan, "half of us will go out with our plough and find the best ploughland in the island. We can't leave here till we take in at least one harvest. The other six will go out to that skerry and throw a net into the sea. We'll have to live on fish till we mill our first oats."

The island from the shore to the summit of the hill Fea was dead and leprous. The land was mottled with black and yellow scabs. The net was dragged in empty time after time, dripping with green stinking scum.

Brendan went to the rock that oozed water. A silver drop hung from his finger end. He put it to his lips. His tongue and lips burned like acid.

The old man came back just before sunset to the cave.

"Are you still here?" he grumbled. "I told you to clear off. Do you expect an old done man to dance attendance on you? You're barking up the wrong tree. Here, take this and be off with you in the morning . . ." He set down the pot of water, and the loaf, and glared at them, and stumped off, with the otter flowing after him.

"It's like David playing on his harp, to hear the guardian speak," said Brendan.

The brothers began to tear bits from the loaf. "Haven't you been warned since you were small boys against the sin of gluttony?" cried Brendan. "Put the pieces of bread back on the plate. There's Matins to say first."

After they had recited Matins, and broken their fast, Brendan said, "We might have to wait till next spring – maybe for a year or two – till the island is fertile again. That was the vow we took. A few years – what are they but grains of sand through an hour-glass?"

Every day the old man came with a jar of water and a loaf, morning and evening, and growled and went away again, with his attendant otter.

Eight times a day the sea wanderers raised hands and voices in adoration and thankfulness. And land and sea brought forth only barrenness. Even at Easter, earth and sea lay shrouded and bound, with the wounds of death on them.

*

Seventy years – seventy grains of sand – seem to be a complete and satisfying number – blessed by the Psalmist – but death when it comes is always a bitter thing. Even for philosophers and poets, the sand as it whorls down to its last few grains, seems but the dust of dead blossoms; and our bones at last get blown about the deserts, hither and thither; and the end, like all else under the sun, is vanity.

Brendan reckoned that the monks were in the island for seventy years.

Not all of them. Some died, one year or another. Brother Paul fell over the cliff one spring, hoping there might be a whitemaa's nest on one of the ledges. (How wonderful an egg would have tasted, in the monotony of their endless bread and water!) It was foolishness, no gull or crow or lark or swan had been seen on the island.

They had managed to make after a time a little convent of stones, with a chapel, and they buried Brother Paul inside the chapel. The old man appeared at the requiem, but came in no further than the threshold. As the last psalm died away, the brothers heard his grumbles. "Gulls' eggs – what a fool!"

And Brother Liam, swinging the net at too wide an arc from the rock, fell into the rotted sea, and he was dead when they drew him in.

There was a good silence when the brothers got up in the morning, but one morning there was a deeper silence from the bed where Brother Emon slept. They looked into his face. He had fallen into the deep silence of death.

The years passed. Silver threads appeared in the beards of those monks who (apart from Brendan) had been hardly more than boys when they came to the island. Here there was a twisted hand – a purblind eye – a head as bald as an egg – a cracked voice – a stone in an ear – a knot in knee or shoulder. The sands were dropping faster and faster through the hour-glass. But a face shone like a boy's at Matins or Vespers, from time to time, even in the storms and blizzards of winter.

The only man who did not change in the island was the provider of water and bread, who turned up grumbling twice a day.

"We're growing old," said Malachi. "but that old complainer, he hasn't aged by an hour since first we came. If anything, he looks younger."

"Angels don't know anything about time," said Brendan. "I hope he brings a big sack of peats tonight. It's been snowing all day. . ."

One day the following spring Brendan the abbot, feeling his way along the rockface, set his fingers on the rock spring that had burned his mouth at the time of their first landfall. The water did not sting his hand. He touched his forefinger to his mouth. "The water is sweet and pure!" he cried.

All the monks came, as fast as they could by reason of age and infirmity. They scooped up the water, in handfuls. "Never have I tasted such delight," said Brother Colm. And the other monks agreed. Nectar and wine were as nothing in comparison.

A week later Brother Flann, coming back from the ruined sheepfold, noticed that a few green sprigs were pushing through the dead earth. "There could be cattle and sheep and cornstalks in this island in a little while," he said. Though he had a rheumaticky knee, Flann almost danced back to the chapel, so eager he was to tell Brendan and the brothers about the green shoots.

The old man stood at the door of the refectory; it was a crude ruckle of stones. "I have bad news for you," he said. "The people are coming back. I saw smoke last night from Norday and Selskay, the islands out there. They'll be here, in this island, before summer's done. They'll soon get rid of idle drones like you. You're a nuisance as far as they're concerned. It's back to the old greed and lust and gluttony and sloth and pride and rage. The ancient wheel is going to give another turn."

"Deo gratias," said Brendan.

"Well," said the old man of the island, "it's all one, as far as I'm concerned. There's no rest for me. I've been here for six or seven turns of the wheel. I've seen it all before."

"I know," said Brendan. "Next time, though, they'll know better."

"Maybe," said the old man, and gave a snort that was half scorn and half laughter. "I wouldn't like to bet on it. You might be right. They had a hard lesson last time."

"You've been very good to us," said Brendan.

The few brothers nodded.

"Peat-time again," said the old man. "I think this is the last time I cut peats for you lot. It's cold out on the ocean. Ancients like you should have a fire amidships."

A month later, the eagle eye of Brother Colm (he could see like a hawk through crystal though he was ninety years old) saw a boat full of young people out in the sound, fishing between two islands. Their faces were young and fresh. They raised hands in greeting to Brother Colm.

Brother Colm went back to the chapel. "They're young strong beautiful people," he said. "They're black. They'll make the islands fertile again. Deo Gratias." The brothers clapped their hands with joy.

The old man of the island came stumbling up over the rocks dripping with sea silver. He threw down two fish on the stones. "Here's a surprise for you," he said. I caught a score of haddocks this morning. This is my first haul of fish for a hundred years. I'll smoke some for you. You'll be glad of them on the ocean. You've worked pretty hard, I must say. Well, I'll not be looking after you any more, you drones. Goodbye."

And he actually kissed Brendan and the five remaining brothers.

And Brendan and the brothers wept.

One morning a month later Brendan and his monks launched their ship and sailed west in search of the Tir-Nan-Og, the Isle of the Ever Young.

Their cargo was a little barrel of water and a few loaves and a few smoked fish, and a sack of peats.

Their ship, though they had neglected it for seventy years, arched through the sea like a dolphin, going west.

In island after island they saw the fires and spades and oxen of the settlers, whose young faces seemed carved out of ebony.

Photograph by Gunnie Moberg

George Mackay Brown

Ikey the Tinker: His Rosary

In Papay I got a fish
From a girl at a croft.
What man in a white coat was crossing the hill?

The lass in a boat for Westray.
A silver-haired wife
Waits on the loud shore stones.

Why so far from home
In Kirkwall, at Yule,
Colder than Ikey, three lost lairds ... ?

Who had seen this before,
The old minister
Star-tongued at his font, in Rinansay?

Many a Hamnavoe boy, at Lammas
Has wandered from school
Among Baltic masts and cordage.

*

A cave under a cliff.
One candle - sleep - then
Lanterns, dogs, guns.

Ikey, the beak's sentenced you
Seven times - oh, more.
You know what happens in a jail.

Ikey, you've gone with ballads
At Gallowsha
For a capful of pennies.

I wait at the kirkyard gates
From Rousay to Hoy
To see, will there be a wake?

*

A man broke bread in a Birsay inn
To two travellers.
"We've seen the Lord of the Harvest."

Who's at the Hoy shore, by starlight
Simmering two fish?
The King of Stars and Oceans.

All roadside dreams! I saw
A ship in Scapa
With a cargo of white birds.

What strangers are you
Among the scattered
Stones in Papay? "Tredwell ... Boniface ..."

A kirk of new stone, in Sanday
A bell nods and cries
Our Lady, Star of the Sea.

The First Daffodil: A Tinker Wife

Dead grass whispers under my feet.
I am going from croft to farm
With my pack - needles, cotton reels,
Tin mugs, cheap hankies

I am going past dog-barkings,
Mockery of a bairn, a tree
Of starlings shaken like a bell.
Sometimes a farm lass

Buys a trinket, often enough
I'm given the hard door, but
A kind one here and there
Pours me a mug of tea.

(I can tell their fortunes too. A few
Suffer a heartfall when I frown.)
Dead dry grass between the crofts
Of Quoy and Seatter,

But last month my boots squelched mud
Along that track. On Greenay side
Boys are lighting fires
- The muirburn - to clean the hill

Of winter's dregs. Sit in the ditch,
Old woman, sit in the ditch.
Strike match into pipe. Another flame
In the wind, over there, a March daffodil.

Salto the Fisherman

Listen, I'm a fisherman. My boat
Is the "Sarah Ann".
I go out on the Atlantic most days.

Salto they call me. "Salto
Ought to be in a big boat with a crew of five ..."
Salto sails out, the last loner.

Salto and "Sarah Ann". We know
All about sudden storms.
We know all about blindness and fogs.

A long salt tarry line
Of fish-lore rooted in the kirkyard
Ties me to moon weathers, the fishless or fish-fraught

Wheel of the wind, the gull check
Over a hidden shoal, the dangerous
Words not to be spoken out west.

I turn the boat for home at sunset.
There's Marjory on the pier.
The gossips, "Salto, when's he going to marry that poor lass?"

Salto doesn't want to leave any widow.
I never eat fish myself.
"Marjory, are the tatties on? Yes,

Sausages and scones, I'm hungry" ...
A middling catch only.
My oilskin gleams like black armour in the lamplight.

A Quest for Geordie

To the Memory of George Mackay Brown

Stanley Robertson

A gaitherin storm wis startin tae streek across the sky an wee Geordie's een wis fair aglow. As he looked at the grey mottled cloods fusing wi the jet black yins, he kent that Thor wisnae far awa. Ay, Geordie could see aa the omens wis there. Thor must hae left Valhalia tae come an snoop upon his very special favourite Orkneys. It wisnae the first time nor wid it be the last that Geordie saa Thor's ill tricks in the sky. The wee boy looked wi awe an wonderment an waited for the sparks tae fly.

His breath wis steamin up the wee windae he wis lookin through an he kept dichtin the windae wi his sark sleeve. Then at last he saa Thor on the back of his giant albatross an settle doon upon the green earth an intae his strang hands wis his huge muckle haimmer. It looked as if it wis made o bronze, wi a michty haunnle, wi a great big heid on it an there wis a shairp pint tae it as weel. Wi a michty thump upon the grun Thor gar the earth tae reel an the scud shook as the land roon aboot. Then Geordie saa Thor tak oot his suppie kindlin an wi makin sparks fly aff his haimmer he startit tae licht the fire. Blue sparks an fire ends started tae flee aroon the Heavens an whit a braw show it gied. Jist as the flames o Thor's fires lit up the cloods, then nae sooner did the rain dance doon in dazzlin deluges upon the droothie earth. The grun fair parched for a drink swallaed up the dram. Aa the clamminess o the evening wint awa leavin only Thor's magic in the air. Geordie wis fair tickled wi aathing.

"O if only I hid the pouer o Thor's haimmer? Geordie thocht. "I could mak folk sit up an listen tae mi. I wid nae langer be a wee laddie but a man o micht. If I can fin oot the pouer o Thor's haimmer there's nae huddin back the things I could dae." Muckle thochts wint roon the boy's mind. Next mornin Geordie wint oot for a ramble roon aboot the Orkneys an he saa a doze o silver-backit seals. Some were on the land an ithers intae the sea. The laddie walked up bravely tae them but maist o them wint intae the waater except yin. Noo this lanely silver-backit seal wis nae ordinary seal. Geordie kent that it wis a silkie.

Speakin tae the silkie Geordie says: "Tell mi aboot the magic o Thor's haimmer cos I ken ye silkies hae the knowledge o aa the magic."

Turnin roon her heid she gently replied, "I am a cratur o the sea mair nor o the land an whin Thor strikes his haimmer I mak for the sea. But yi will persist aboot the magic oo the haimmer then gang an ask the Auld Man o Hoy, wha nae only kens the sea magic but also the magic o Thor's haimmer."

Geordie thanked the silkie an ran tae see the Auld Man o Hoy. On reachin the Auld Man o Hoy Geordie looked up tae his tousled heid that wis covered wi mosses an lickens an shouts, "Auld Sodjer, ye wha sits guardin the shores o Orkneys, I ask a boon o ye."

Withoot a voice Geordie could hear the wirdies come frae the Auld Man o Hoy. "Ye're fairly richt, laddie, for I hae bin the sentinel guaird here for sic a lang time. Fine dae I ken whin things gae wrang in the sea or on the land. Mi feet are plantit intae the waaters an the fish lick mi taes an tell mi aa but even though the birds nestle upon mi bonnet I can see aathin that gangs on abune the waves. Monies the time I hae watched Thor come doon an cause ill tricks upon the Orkneys. Whit dis a wee laddie like ye want wi Thor?"

"I want tae ken the pouer o Thor's Haimmer cos I want tae hae sic muckle pouer as weel an command respec frae folks whin I become a man."

Then replied The Auld Man o Hoy, "Weel, ask him yersel cos he comes here again the mornin. For jist afore midnicht staund upon the wee lummock jist afore yer hoose an whin Thor comes doon ask him yersel. Mind ye, laddie, Thor can be gey formidable."

Geordie thanked the wise Auld Man O Hoy an wint back tae his hoose an waited patiently for the late hours tae approach. Then the appointed time drew near an Geordie wint oot an sat upon the wee lummock jist ootside his hoose. The late nicht wisnae ower clammy but aa the signs o Thor were there. Aifter a whilie Thor cam doon frae the Heavens upon his giant albatross an he settled doon in front o the lummock. Wee Geordie wisnae feart an undaunted he said, "Great Warrior, Thor, tell mi the magic an pouer o yer pouerfu haimmer."

Thor gied a loud laugh. "Fit wid ye want tae dae wi mi haimmer?"

"I wid like tae ken hou tae command respec an tae mak folks sit up an listen tae mi."

"But laddie, ye couldnae lift mi haimmer nor neither could onybody else for that maitter. Geordie, I cannae gie ye the pouer o mi haimmer but I can gie ye the pouer o respec. But even gin I help ye hou tae get it, mind ye it still must be earned. Ay, laddie, respec maun aye be earned."

Thor wint tae his great albatross an pu'ed oot a tail feather an gied it tae Geordie. Let mi tell ye that this feather is mair pouerfu sometimes than mi haimmer is."

Geordie couldna unnerstaun hou a feather could be mair pouerfu nor the haimmer but Thor reassured the laddie that it wis so.

"Hou dae I uise it, great Thor?" Geordie asked.

Thor answered, "Dip it in ink." Then Thor wint awa again on his albatross. Geordie wint hame an dipped his pen intae the ink an pittin it tae paper fand he wis able tae write better nor he'd ever deen afore. Perhaps he didnae hae the pouer o the haimmer but he fand the pouer o the pen. Geordie grew up an wint tae universities an got aa kind o great merits an honours. Why his feather an his ain creativity could mak the auld norse legends come alive. Nae wunner the Auld Man O Hoy could speak tae him, cos he nae only spoke, an wrote, but he listened. Geordie became a great man leavin the warld a bonnie legacy o the wirdies o wisdom.

So gin ony o ye folks ever look up tae the Auld Man o Hoy an see what ye may think is a giant bird, weel, ye may be wrang cos I think it is perhaps Geordie sittin on tap wi his feather an ink recording the events an history o his maist beloved Orkneys.

George Mackay Brown, a dear freen, an a magic wirdsmith.

'Hamnavoe Revisited'
An Interview With George Mackay Brown
William Sharpton

George Mackay Brown was born in Stromness, Orkney in October 1921. He was the youngest of five children to John and Mhairi (Mackay) Brown. He attended Newbattle Abbey, in Dalkeith, when Edwin Muir was Warden. He graduated from the University of Edinburgh in 1960, with a degree in English Literature. Brown has written ten volumes of poetry, six novels and seven collections of short stories, also several plays, essays and children's books. Sir Peter Maxwell Davies, world renowned composer who lives on Hoy, collaborated with Brown on several projects, setting his poetry to music. The 1994 Saint Magnus Festival in Orkney premiered several compositions based upon Brown's writing. A new joint work, *The Three Kings*, an adaption of several Christmas poems, made its world debut in October 94 at London's Barbican Concert Hall.

In January 1974, GMB was awarded an OBE. He received honorary degrees from Dundee University (Ll.D) and Glasgow University (D.Litt). In 1987, he received the James Tait Black Memorial Prize for his novella, *The Golden Bird*. His recent novel, *Beside the Ocean of Time* (John Murray), was short-listed for the Booker Prize and received the Saltire Award for Scottish Book of the Year in 1994. A new book of short stories *Winter Tales* and one of poetry, *Following a Lark* has just appeared.

[This interview with WS took place in early July 1994, in Stromness.]

WS: How much of an influence were Edwin and Willa Muir on your writing, while at Dalkeith? Did they have an inspirational effect on you?
GMB: Yes, they did. They were very encouraging. It was the first time I'd ever had any real encouragement. There weren't many students at Newbattle when I was there, so Edwin had time to deal individually with students. We were required to submit an essay, once a month or so, which could be interpreted very loosely. You could send in a poem, a story or a piece of autobiography. Edwin would discuss it with you afterwards. I think I must have sent in two or three poems. In the end he sent a poem of mine to the *New Statesman* and they printed it. I was delighted about that because I never dreamed of having a poem in such an august magazine. He also sent a poem to *The Listener*. He was very good that way. In fact, it was Edwin who gathered some of the poems I'd written and sent them to Hogarth Press. I didn't know anything about it till I received a letter from a lady called Mrs Smallwood [managing director at Hogarth] a year or two later. She said she would like to make a book of them. And that's how things began.
WS: You have stated that growing up between the wars was a very bleak time for a child in Stromness. Could you comment on that?
GMB: Well, in a way it was. It was a rather depressed period -- socially

and economically. But when you're a child, poverty doesn't mean every-thing just as long as you are happy. So it wasn't really a bad period at all. I look back on it with great pleasure.

WS: Was there ballad-singing and music at home when you were a child?

GMB: My father [local postman, tailor] had quite a good tenor voice. But all he sang were Edwardian music hall ballads, the things he used to sing when he was a young man – evangelical hymn tunes.

WS: Did your older sister [Ruby], parents or relations tell you many stories?

GMB: Well, there was plenty of talk around the piers among the fishermen. They would tell stories. But my sister, she was a profound influence. She was ten years older than me – when I was five, she was fifteen – and would tell me stories, usually love stories. They were rather sad stories because usually one of them died or got killed or drowned on the way to the love tryst. She would always end the stories in a ritual way, saying, "and then she died of a broken heart." [Laughter.] When you're five years old, you don't know what this love business is. But I was enthralled by that. Ruby was a very good storyteller. It established a kind of rhythm in the imagination.

WS: When you were a schoolboy, did you read many books?

GMB: I didn't read many books actually. But every week there came a boy's magazine from a firm in Dundee called D.C. Thomson – the Wizard, the Hotspur and The Rover. All the boys read these magazines. They were frowned on by our teachers and parents. Oh, well, I really didn't have any literary models at all.

WS: What are the happiest moments you recollect from your childhood, growing up here in Stromness?

GMB: We played football a lot. I was good at football, too. [pause] There was just wandering around the hills and the shores, and bathing in the sea. And the long summer holidays. Of course, when you look back, every day was brimming with sunshine, which can't have been the case at all. You just remember the good days and bury all the other ones. So I was quite happy as a child, really.

WS: Did you do any fishing at all?

GMB: No. I didn't have any skill of that sort. The worst thing that hap-pened to me in childhood was that we began to smoke, about the age of twelve. Smoke cheap cigarettes. We didn't think of it at the time, but what they say is true. It's a killer. Because it actually ruined my health. I was discovered to have TB when I was nineteen. But I think it had started a few years before that. Suddenly, I was no longer able to play football and run around. I began to suffer from depression and that. So I think smok-ing. . . it almost killed me, that's for sure.

WS: What first inspired you to start writing poetry?

GMB: I don't know. I think it was just bred in the bones, somehow. I sup-pose everybody has a gift of some kind, as it says in Scripture.

WS: When did you first read *The Hound of Heaven* [Francis Thompson]?

GMB: Oh, I must have been fifteen or sixteen. I was very impressed with it. Great stuff. I don't think it's quite so good now as I'd remember it, but that doesn't matter. The impression it made at that time is what counts.

WS: What drew your attention to the *Orkneyinga Saga*, and writing about Magnus?

GMB: That was the natural one to read, the *Orkneying Saga*. I started reading it when I was seventeen. I thought it was wonderful. I've read it several times since then. And the story of Magnus, I thought was the best part of all. The conflict between these two men (cousins) and the death of Magnus. . . everything that followed. I was enthralled by it, and still am. [Pause.] And I loved the narrative flow, without any extraneous material. It's a pure narrative line all the way.

WS: Where there any poets in the 1940's-50's that you enjoyed?

GMB: Oh yes, there were a few. Eliot and Yeats, of course. Auden and Spender. Dylan Thomas – a disastrous man to imitate. But I liked some of his work very much indeed. These, and Muir, were major influences.

WS: Are there any contemporary poets in Scotland whom you enjoy?

GMB: Yes, there are some very good ones like [Norman] MacCaig and Iain Crichton Smith. There's not all that many when you come to think about it. There is a young chap in Edinburgh called Brian McCabe. Do you know his work? He's very, very good. But a lot of these younger poets don't seem to want to go through the trouble to learn the craft, you know. They just slap down a few lines of raw emotion on the page. That's not poetry at all. It's just a mess. It is a long apprenticeship that has to be gone through. You have got to learn how to write sonnets, different kinds of stanzas – Spenserian, Burns stanzas, ballads and all that sort of thing. These younger ones don't want to know about that. Just lurch a few words on the page. Four-letter words especially spiced-in there. That's a poem?. . . dreadful.

WS: When you write a poem or a story, do you see the entire piece as a whole or as one image?

GMB: It comes as one image. Either it develops from there or it falls on stoney soil.

WS: Did the tuberculosis affect your writing?

GMB: I can't remember doing much writing. I read quite a bit and listened to music a lot. I wasn't desperately ill. I wasn't lying in bed for six months at a time or anything like that. Sometimes I think, looking back, this recurrent illness is a kind of refuge. When things are beginning to be too much, you suddenly become ill. Not desperately ill, but ill enough to avoid your responsibilities. And you're out of the game for six months or a year, or something like that. It's very strange how the mind works. It can suggest to you that you're ill - but the physical symptoms are there too, of course.

WS: Regarding Seamus Heaney, you hold him in high esteem as a poet. Are there any other poets in the last twenty-five years that you admire?

GMB: Well there is [Ted] Hughes, the poet laureate. I liked some of his earlier poems very much. And there is Iain Crichton Smith in Scotland. And who else? There's not all that many, I'm sorry to say. I think as you get older, you lose your appetite for poetry.

WS: Are you working on any new poems?

GMB: I was very busy last year [1993]. I wrote about twenty poems – there might be a book of poems next year, and a book of short stories, too. It's the only thing I can do, you see. I sit here in the morning and would be bored stiff if I didn't have that to do. I really would!! That is the happiest time of the day, when I'm sitting in my little kitchen after breakfast, writing for two or three hours. I like that.

WS: What was the poet's pub (Milne's) like when you were living in Edinburgh in the late 50's-early 60's?

GMB: It was a wonderful place – a great bar. All the writers and artists used to meet there. It wasn't a beautiful place but the staff were good. So we use to meet there every Friday evening and Saturday. Sometimes the great bard himself, Hugh MacDiarmid, would appear from Lanarkshire.

WS: Were you taken with MacDiarmid's poetry?

GMB: The early poetry very much, including *The Drunk Man Looks At The Thistle*. But after that it was terrible. I couldn't read them.

WS: Did you meet Norman MacCaig or Sorley MacLean?

GMB: I didn't meet Sorley, he was teaching somewhere in the west. But there is another very neglected poet called Sydney Goodsir Smith who wrote in Scots. It was strange because he spoke in a kind of Oxford English, and he wrote in dense Scots. He was a very good poet – and a good man, too. I liked him.

Many Friday evenings after the pubs closed at ten o'clock, MacCaig would have an impromptu party at his house. There were some great parties up there, lasting till about three o'clock in the morning. His wife (Isabel) was so kind and tolerant. Imagine a housewife having a quiet evening at home, reading a book or listening to the radio and a dozen men all merry with beer busting in on her serenity. But she welcomed everybody. So kind.

WS: How were the Fifties for you?

GMB: I enjoyed the University. It was great. I studied English Literature. I didn't get terribly much out of that but I enjoyed the language part of it – the Old English. After grasping the key, the grammar, I thought it was wonderful! Getting to the roots of the language. Quite fascinating.

WS: When you were at University were you also writing poetry? Some of the pieces that appeared in *Loaves And Fishes?*

GMB: I can't remember writing any poetry when I was in Edinburgh. It was when I came back to Orkney that the poems began to flow again. I always thought that I would come back to Stromness because I liked it here best of all. I could work here, and I could write here better than anywhere else. But I knew everybody, you know. It was a real home for me.

WS: When you converted to Roman Catholicism [in 1961], was that a major event? Did that have an impact on your writing?

GMB: Yes, but I had been thinking about it for fifteen or sixteen years. It never had any catastrophic impact on the way I thought or believed, because it had been there so long. The interest was sparked off by an anti-Catholic essay by Lytton Strachey, one of the Bloomsbury group. I was enthralled by that essay and the history of the Roman Church.

WS: In your book of poetry, *The Year of the Whale*, what inspired 'The Seven Houses' about John Fitzgerald Kennedy? What made an Orcadian write about the assassination of an American President?

GMB: I can't remember – of course the whole world was shocked. I suppose it was because he was young, and we thought he was going to do great things. The terrible end of it all was so shocking. But I don't think it was a good poem, because I can't remember anything about it; it was probably written too near the event.

WS: Aside from Kennedy, I know you wrote a wonderful piece, 'The Burning Harp,' for Neil Gunn.

GMB: Oh, yes. It was for his eightieth birthday. I wrote a tiny story, only about four pages long and written in a saga style. When I was young, in my teens, I read *Morning Tide* and was absolutely enchanted by it. I'm not so keen on him now. There is a kind of mystical element that comes into it, but it doesn't work for me somehow. There was another Orcadian novelist about the same time called Eric Linklater. He inspired one or two of us young Orcadians. He has a beautiful style, but he is disregarded nowadays, forgotten almost. But I think his time will come back again.

WS: Did you meet Linklater?

GMB: Yes, twice. but I can't remember much about him. I think we were both slightly tipsy at the time, so we didn't say anything very profound to each other.

WS: How about, Orcadian writer-poet, Robert Rendall. Did you know him?

GMB: Yes, I knew him very well. He was a draper in Kirkwall. He was stone deaf when I met him, but that didn't seem to affect his life at all. You could hold a very good conversation with him and he seemed to know what you were saying to him. When he was in his late forties-early fifties he began to write short poems in the Orkney dialect, wonderful poems. He also wrote poems in English and sonnets, but they weren't so good. The Orkney dialect poems were beautiful. I think they were probably better than anything Muir and myself have written.

WS: Robert Frost once said, "I don't like to write anything I don't see." Do you feel this is accurate in application to your own poetry?

GMB: No, it doesn't apply to me at all. I write my best things about experiences that I've never had and things that I have never seen. I think poetry is different; you can't lay down strict laws that you must write poetry about *this*, in this fashion. Everybody must plough his own furrow, as they say. But strangely enough, Robert Frost's grandmother came from the island of Hoy. Edwin Muir went to America to do the Charles Eliot Norton lectures at Harvard University and met Frost there. They got on very well together.

WS: Frost's grandmother came from Hoy?

GMB: From the isle of Hoy. And there is another famous American writer [Washington Irving] that wrote *Rip Van Winkle*. His father came from an island, near Kirkwall, called Shapinsay. That's very interesting because that famous story is based on an Orkney folk legend about the fiddler who disappears for twenty-five years (in some versions it is a century) and is taken underground by the fairy people. He comes back and is still the same age as when he disappeared but everything has changed. I think Washington Irving must have heard that story in his cradle and it comes out as *Rip Van Winkle*.

WS: Have Orcadian and Norse folk tales influenced your writing?

GMB: Oh yes, they have. First, I wrote a book for children of the Orkney folk tales. I embroidered it, you know. I didn't stick to the basic stories. I tarted them up to make them palatable for late twentieth century children. It is a book called *The Two Fiddlers*. That is the same story as *Rip Van Winkle*.

WS: What about the fiddlers? There are a lot of fiddlers throughout your work.

GMB: There are a lot of fiddlers in Orkney, but they are mostly in the country districts. There were one or two in Stromness, but I don't remember them ever coming to our house and playing. And really, I wasn't interested in music at all.

WS: Have you written ghost stories?

GMB: I've never had any supernatural experiences in my life. I have never seen a ghost. In fact, if one walked through that wall now I would probably die of fright! But there was a publishing firm called Barrie & Jenkins who used to put out a book every Christmas called *The Ghost Book*. The editor wrote to me for a ghost story in early 70s. So, I wrote a ghost story. I can turn up these stories to order; I don't have to wait for 'inspiration'. Then, for the next seven or eight years, I wrote a ghost story every year for this anthology.

WS: What inspired the short story 'Witch' you wrote about Marion Isbister?

GMB: She was a kind of composite person, Marion Isbister. There was a whole crop of these witches about the beginning of the seventeenth century. It was a terrible story because they were all executed in Kirkwall.

WS: Was this about the time of King James VI?

GMB: Around that time, yes. It was nearly all women (being persecuted) in Orkney – and James's cousins were the earls. Terrible times.

WS: Did you know [Orcadian folklorist] Ernest Marwick?

GMB: Oh yes, I knew him very well. He was a great man, Ernest, and left behind a great mass of papers and manuscripts when he died that have just been slowly put together now and published. There is one volume, but there are more to come.

WS: [Robert] Frost once stated that if an epitaph were written on his stone it would say, "I had a lover's quarrel with the world." If you were to look upon your literary life, what would you consider for your epitaph?

GMB: Oh . . . [Laughter.] I hadn't thought about that. That was an interesting thing for Frost to say. Some things about life I like very much. Other things I wouldn't like to experience again, to tell you the truth. I have just been reading a new biography of Robert Louis Stevenson and he wrote that beautiful epitaph of himself. 'Under the Wide and Starry Sky'. It ends,

'This be the verse you grave for me/ Here he lies where he longed to be/ Home is the sailor, home from sea/ And the hunter home from the hill.'

He was an Edinburgh man, of course. His father and his grandfather built lighthouses around the coast. You can see a few in Grimsay, on that little island just out there. The Stevensons built all these lighthouses. They were wonderful engineers. I think Robert Louis must have broken his father's heart because he didn't go in for that at all. He veered off in another direction, which the elder Stevenson(s) must have regarded with deep suspicion. All this business of poetry, story-telling and that. Not in accordance with the strict Presbyterian ethos.

WS: Did you read much of Stevenson when you were in school?

GMB: No, I didn't really. Some boys were enthralled by *Treasure Island* and *Kidnapped.* Somehow I never got the taste for it, but liked his poems.

WS: He wrote *A Child's Garden of Verses.* Have you written verse for children?

GMB: Not really. I do write birthday acrostics. You write the name down, and the poems flow from their names. That keeps me quite busy.

WS: Oscar Wilde once said, "one's real life is, so often, the life that one does not lead." If you had not followed the path where you became a writer-poet, what do you envision you would have done with your life?

GMB: That's very profound when you think about it. [Pause.] I can't really imagine. I probably would have ended up a clerk in some bank or office or something. I wouldn't be any good as a fisherman or farmer. I tried teaching once near Edinburgh. It was a dreadful experience, shocking. I decided that God had not called me to be a teacher. Then I had one of my attacks of illness and the knew it was the end of my teaching career. I said, "Oh, no, it's too bad for my health. I couldn't possibly be a teacher."

WS: Who had been the most important influence on your life? Was it your mother, or your dad . . . or someone else?

GMB: I don't know who was the most important. Certainly both my parents were. I think they were inclined to spoil me a bit, being the youngest of the family. I don't ever remember being hit or physically abused. They were very kind to me, maybe too kind; however, that is what happens in families.

WS: Did you read James Frazer's *The Golden Bough?*

GMB: No. These enormous tomes tend to put me off. I enjoyed poems and Scottish ballads in school. When we were young, we had one period each week for religious instruction. Our teacher read us these wonderful stories – David and Goliath, Joseph and his Brothers, King David – out of the Old Testament. I was absolutely fascinated by these stories. They had a deep effect on me somehow. I think these Hebrew stories are among the greatest stories ever told.

WS: In relationship to these stories and converting to Catholicism, do you think that your gift for writing is a 'God-given' gift?

GMB: I think it is. And when you think about it, nearly everybody can do something rather well. It is extraordinary, but it's a shame that there should be this hierarchy of talents. A writer's regarded as being better than a man who builds stone walls or a carpenter. I don't like all these distinctions, because they are all really craftsmen in their own way. 'Makars' in the Old Scots. I hate all that artistic snobbery and try to defuse it whenever I come across it.

WS: Is the use of numerology, within your prose and poetry, by design? For instance, the use of the number seven.

GMB: Seven ways of looking at one event or subject. It seems to me to be almost the perfect number, you know, to establish a work of art. Giving it this seven-fold shape.

WS: What made you first decide to include Hamnavoe into your writing?

GMB: Hamnavoe is the old name of the village. It was the original name. and Stromness was the parish round about. Finally, they decided that Stromness was the official name. I think it was a pity because Hamnavoe is such a lovely, descriptive name. Old Norse, meaning *haven inside the bay*.

WS: Do you think there is a future for poetry?

GMB: I don't think it looks bright at the moment. Far from it. Maybe it is just diving underground, but it will come up again. You can't kill it, but they are doing their best. Technology is the great enemy. And these kids have taken to it like ducks to water. I have no intention of ever doing that. I'll just stick to my old paper and pen. There is something about writing, you know. The rhythm of it is compatible with the human mind and imagination.

WS: When the literary world and posterity look back on your work, what would you like them to remember about your work?

GMB: [Laughter.] I don't really care. They will just take what they want, I suppose. But there it is ... and it has been good fun. I have enjoyed writing very much. I was so glad to be given that one talent, because there is nothing else I can do very well.

In Memorium George Mackay Brown

The Reception of his Work in German

Esther Garke

When the German language newspapers - especially Swiss ones in Berne and Zurich - related George Mackay Brown's unexpected and quiet passing on 13 April 1996, his readers here - like Scotland's literary community - mourned the loss of a great and fascinating writer. As a homage to G M Brown (GMB as he is affably called) the Swiss radio hastened to broadcast (on 24 April) some of his best known poems (such as the 'Sea Runes' and those on 'Rackwick,' 'Hoy') set to music by Peter Maxwell Davies.

It may seem surprising that this Scottish writer from the remote Orkney Islands is held in such high esteem in Switzerland. In a perfunctory manner this may be explained by the fact that GMB's friend and literary agent from John Murray Publishers, London, Hugo Brunner, has Swiss ancestors and has always been most helpful in establishing useful contacts; it is furthermore due to the Swiss publishing house, Verlag Im Waldgut (CH-8500 Frauenfeld*) which, in 1990, meritoriously began to publish the German translations of GMB's work, after the Swiss and Austrian radio stations had broadcast recitals of some of GMB's short stories, and after two Swiss papers and a literary magazine (*ZeitSchrift/Reformatio*, Berne) had printed a few of his poems and stories. The editor of Verlag Im Waldgut, Beat Brechbühl - himself a well known Swiss poet and novelist, and as much averse to grandiloquence as GMB used to be - was immediately spellbound by GMB's short stories, poems and novels when he first read them. Recognizing at once their great literary quality, he did not hesitate to publish a collection of Christmas Stories (*Weihnachtsgäste*), followed by four translated novels (*Vinland, The Golden Bird, Beside the Ocean of Time, Greenvoe*) and a collection of poems in a hand-set bibliophile edition in autumn 1996*; ready for publication in the years to come are the manuscripts of the German translations of *Magnus* as well as some of the collections of short stories (*Andrina, The Masked Fisherman, Winter Tales**).

I take it as a great privilege and am grateful for the chance to translate the work of this extraordinary, congenial writer and wonderful, gentle person. I first came across his work thirty years ago; I then corresponded with him for two decades before finally his Swiss editor and myself got at last the chance to meet George in Stromness and to spend a brilliant summer solstice with him – an unforgettable day. George was always most helpful when there was a problem with the translation say of an idiom or an image; and how we did laugh when we tried in competition to locate the sources of one of his literary allusions or biblical quotations!

Nowadays both English and German literature seem to be animated and invigorated by their fringes, by authors from peripheral regions – from Scotland and the islands in the North on the one hand, from the Alpine regions in the South and Southeast on the other. Maybe there is a secret congeniality between the Swiss and the Scots, the "brother mountaineers" (as Professor Hans Utz from the University of Berne calls them in his monograph *Schotten und Schweizer*, Berne 1995). Though generalisations are misleading and often fallacious, it cannot be denied that both the Swiss and the Scots share certain traditions: a tradition of herdsmen who like fisherman lead a life of simplicity, with a deep respect for the supremacy of a predominant, unsentimentally crude nature, dependence on which makes itself felt every day, providing a hotbed for superstitious beliefs in trolls, gnomes and fairies. The farmers' and fishermen's dependence on each other taught them to enjoy and endure life in small communities. Their remoteness on the islands or in the mountains helped to engender a longstanding tradition of myths, sagas, and legends. Both countries have a strong Protestant tradition; both have had to put up with mighty neighbours – there the English in 1745; here the Hapsburg dynasty first, then the French in 1798; both use their language and dialects to distinguish themselves from their neighbours. Their being rooted in their natural surroundings, in the sterile soil of their land, may have contributed to a certain steadfastness; and their staunch, firm, unflinching and unyielding character is in a way reflected in their literatures. All these features, which characterise also GMB's protagonists, may have led the Swiss readers to a feel a certain affinity with him and his work, with his themes and his style.

These and other traits of GMB's writing have been evoked in German, Austrian and Swiss reviews: the *Neue Zürcher Zeitung* emphasized his orginality, his working outside the mainstream, "beside the ocean of time" so to speak; the *Süddeutsche Zeitung* referred to the integrity of a worldrenowned novelist who holds up a mirror to the whole world by concentrating on his local island; the Bernese *Bund* pointed out GMB's unpretentious, unrefined and pithy language, the Literary Supplement of the Swiss weekly *Weltwoche* had the headline "Trouvaille," a happy discovery, when reviewing GMB's *Beside the Ocean of Time*. German and Swiss reviewers acclaim the fact that when GMB relates the experience of the Orcadians, past and present, he does it in the manner of the story-teller of old, seated by the fireside on a long winter night. Acting the part, as it were, he is proud of the warrior's success, the rebel's exploit, he is sympathetic to the fisherman's struggles and heartbreaks, he feels for the old and lonely, he shares the children's joys, and when (as in the short story 'Gold Dust') he accounts a poet's life among inquisitive, gossiping inhabitants of a small island seaport, he reveals his great sense of humour. His Continental reviewers also applaud GMB's poetic form, which corresponds entirely with his themes, with his notion of the world, with his attitude of mind. He needs no technical tricks, no esoteric symbolism nor learned associations. His style is timeless, clear and unobtrusive. He avoids any artificiality, pose, padding, every insincere mannerism. The beauty of his prose and verse lies in that calm motion of a broad but unaffected mind searching for meaning and truth; this was what made him (what Willie McIlvanney called) an antidote to our present society that believes it was born yesterday and constantly remakes itself.

The Swiss literary community paid homage to GMB on 10 June 1996, when on the publication of the German edition of *Greenvoe* by Waldgut) a reading will take place in Zurich, and later on 23 August 1996 when Erland Brown, George's nephew, will open an exhibition in Küsnacht/Zurich displaying his paintings (including the jackets he designed for his uncle's books published at John Murray's). When I wrote to GMB (also on behalf of the Swiss-British Society) to invite him, possibly together with his Stromness friend and painter Ian MacInnes, to attend the recital in Zürich, he replied in what was to be his last letter – in his usual modest and humorous way that he had never been a great traveller but that he would be with us in spirit and that maybe "a helicopter could take me on the roof of the theatre – a coup de théâtre that would be! ..." And who knows - just as Orkney (to quote Edwin Muir) is a land where the lives of the living people turn into legend, and just as in GMB's stories the wonderful merges with the ordinary, I should not at all be astonished to discover that most unassuming of Orcadian bards sitting there among the audience in Zürich and listening to his poems being read out, the first of which will be in memory of his funeral day - 'April the Sixteenth'...

Verlag Im Waldgut (Chief Editor: Beat Brechbühl), Industriestrasse 21, CH-8500 Frauenfeld, Switzerland where the following books by GM Brown appeared in German translated by Esther Garke:

- *Weihnachtgäste* (Selected Christmas Stories), 1990. 158pp
- *Weinland* (*Vinland*), 1993. 297pp
- *Der Goldene Vogel* (*The Golden Bird*), 1994. 152pp
- *Taugenichts und Dichter Traum* (*Beside the Ocean of Time*), 1995. 191pp
- *Die Greenvoe-Story* (*Greenvoe*), 1996. 283pp
- *Gedichte* (A Selection of Poems), planned for autumn, 1996

Cartoons by "Spike". Reproduced with the permission of the family.

George Mackay Brown:
a 70th birthday celebration

Stewart Conn

A celebration for George Mackay Brown's 70th birthday, arranged by his lifelong friend Archie Bevan, was presented by the Edinburgh Contemporary Arts Trust in the Queen's Hall on 8 December 1991. A selection of the poet's work was spoken and sung. Sir Peter Maxwell Davies played his haunting "Farewell to Stromness". And Stewart Conn was invited to give a personal appreciation. He prefaces it here:

To revise or update this tribute would, I feel, be at odds with the spirit of the original occasion. I simply hope that it may catch something of George, for those who didn't know him; and for those who did, spark off memories of their own. Nor is it a literary assessment: the recent obituaries eloquently served the grandeur of his achievement as a poet and story-teller, and his compassionate involvement with humankind.

In 1994 *Beside the Ocean of Time* was shortlisted for the Booker Prize and won the Saltire Award. George wore this, as he did all laurels and honours, without *hubris*. To the last he was true to his origins; his imagination ever fertile, his insight honed but benign: and all achieved (as those closest to him confirm) with a stoic dedication to his craft; and uncomplaining fortitude in the face of what he knew was drawing near.

Many years ago he wrote a little 'rune': *No more poems / On this island for ever. / The schoolmaster has come.* Now his own pen has been stilled by the coming of the scythe-bearer. But he is still enduringly with us: in the bereftness of his beloved Orkney, as in the wider 'literary' world; his values and vision, preserved in a language as individual as it is uncompromising, as local as universal. We are grateful for the abundance of his gifts, and his use of them.

George Mackay Brown
a birthday tribute

I first visited Orkney in the early Sixties, to make a radio feature. Among those I met were Robert Rendall, sonneteer and collector of shells, or 'grottiebuckies'; the painter Stanley Cursitor, irked at a *Radio Times* misprint describing him not as the Queen's limner but the Queen's *limmer* in Scotland; and an imperturbably cherubic George Mackay Brown, with his mariner's gait and twinkling eye, and impeccable compass-bearing on the nearest pint. Readings from *The Storm* and *Loaves and Fishes* (of whose "strangeness and magic" Edwin Muir had spoken) were added to the recordings already lodged in the BBC sound archive. Some, menaced by sea-water as the St Ola lurched past Hoy, made it by the skin of their teeth; while one tape, recorded after a home brew session (and now probably in the vaults of the University of Buffalo) was found to contain only rhythmic snores.

I've made several trips since: on holiday, for readings, and to discuss the radio productions of *A Spell for Green Corn* and *The Voyage of St Brandon*. I can think of no happier merging of work and pleasure. Whatever the season, Orcadian hospitality swept one off one's feet. And straddling the summer solstice came the Festival. Each year George would gravely welcome his invited poet: Hughes, Heaney, MacCaig, Crichton Smith - a hard act to follow. Self-contained yet eager for news, brimful of impish mimicry and bubbling fun, he would prick the pomposities of the Arts World, enthuse over writers he admired - and unpredictably intone lines from W. B. Yeats. Along with others he has encouraged over the years, I think of him as a bonfire at which to warm the spirit, features glowing; his perceptions illuminating.

There is no deviousness or malice in George. He is as acute in his critical assessments as in his judgment of character. An unblinking directness is equally a hallmark of his own writing - less Scottish than Norse in its inheritance, its saga-like clarity and drive. He uniquely embodies a one-man bardic tradition; his output a wondrous repository of time and place, an almost mediaeval marriage of inspiration and craft. His characters are pared to essentials; with a vibrancy of description and expression which imprints itself on the emotional retina, and resonates in the mind. "Keeping the sources pure" as he puts it, his finest lyrics (often in different colours of biro on multi-coloured paper), have the formal perfection of a rose garden: blooms impeccably pruned but of a profusion and radience inimitably their own.

Many Mackay Brown short stories demonstrate his beloved Hopkins's "naked encounter of sensualism and asceticism". But there's nothing airy-fairy about them. Among their ingredients are violence, lechery and drunkenness. Nor does he lose sight of his characters' primitive hungers, and economic privations - or the mortality that consumes them. And whether conjuring up Bede's "bird in the lighted hall", or Hamnavoe shimmering between fantasy and reality, they emerge vividly from his own impressions and intuition: in the garb of martyr or earl, whaler or tinker-girl, farmer or priest. The protagonists of his novels and dramas too, however timeless or austere their backdrop, remain localised; dependent upon net and plough and vulnerable to the threat of technology, totalitarianism and nuclear disaster over-shadowing our own lives.

Deeply spiritual, all George writes is underpinned by his Catholicism - its liturgy in turn permeated by pagan ritual, incantation and myth. Again, however intricate his symbolism, he retains the common touch; showing compassion for the alcoholic girl, the warrior unmanned, the grieving widow. His values have been furthered through the filming of his work: from *An Orkney Trilogy* to Bill Forsyth's *Andrina*. And he must take pride in having inspired such a range of music, notably from Thomas Wilson and, pre-eminently and exuberantly, Peter Maxwell Davies. The making of music by children too, in a process as seemingly natural as breathing, remains one of the most appealing aspects of the Orkney Festival: creation and achievement of others, but pervaded by and reflecting his presence and personality.

He has achieved international recognition and academic distinction, winning among others the coveted Katherine Mansfield short story award. But there are no flies on him. Before the presentation of an SAC literature prize on TV, he and the other two shortlisted writers met in the greenroom. One suggested that whoever got it, they split the proceeds. The other agreed. George said no. George won! Another time, when we were staying in Glasgow, he was down for a television appearance. We arranged for him to eat with us. When I collected him at his hotel, a plastic and glass monstrosity, we weren't allowed in the bar: it was Sunday, and we hadn't ties on. In due course I left him at the studios, and wished him luck. Next week came a card: "When I got back to the Lorne late that night, hordes of drunken ruffians were being shovelled into the gutter - all wearing ties!"

I've dim memories of him in the Abbotsford, Milne's and Paddy's Bar. Years on, a letter from Orkney hinted at universal custom: dated 31 December it ended, "I must go now. I hear them coming for me." He belongs above all to his environment: the almost treeless landscape and stark seascape he has miraculously transformed, and where he prefers to remain a "word-voyager (who) rarely voyages far from his rocking chair". Even a travel bursary lured him no further than Dublin. He has been deprived of choice latterly by illness: prolonged stays in hospital and, as he graphically put it, "trenched by wounds", periods of recuperation (as now) at home. In the face of this he remains full of concern for others, making light of his own condition and the pain he has borne with fortitude.

His enforced absence makes this evening's presentation of his work, in its authentic cadences, and our shared gratitude towards him, all the more meaningful. He is the most modest and unselfseeking of people, the least ostentatious or opportunist among writers, but rather a man of gritty integrity: a born story-teller who so far from blinding himself to the bleakness of the void has confronted it unflinchingly and unforgettably. More practically, and loyal to those in Stromness who over the years have fondly cared for him, he remains a never po-faced bridger of age and class barriers. In all things he *rings true*. George Mackay Brown is one if the very few people I know whom I believe, in his life as in his art, to be utterly uncorrupted, and uncorruptible. I am proud to say this, and wish him happiness and comfort in the days ahead - not just on my own behalf, but as the mouthpiece of all.

George Mackay Brown Remembered

Margaret Tait

I've been asked as a fellow Orcadian to contribute a note about GMB. On the strength of having read some of his work, but by no means all of it, there's no call for me to attempt an assessment or to add to the many eulogies already in print - so these are just a few remarks, really, no more than that.

His admirable steady perseverance in the occupation of writing, succeeding, in such a precarious profession, to earn his living by it, to win awards and prizes and in fact be a popular author started right from his youth, when he wrote a weekly column - "Island Diary" signed GMB - for the Orkney Herald of those days. I read those with pleasure, whenever I was home in Orkney, so glad to see evidence of a writer in our midst. His pieces were often paralleled by the witty cartoons of "Spike" (Bob Johnston) which frequently depicted a GMB of determined chin, in blown-about mackintosh and long scarf floating in the wind, going about the business of reporting events in the Isles. The long-standing dispute about where to site a new pier for Papa Westray, with strong rival factions in the island having opposite ideas of where it should be, was a recurrent source of fun for those two.

It's not quite true that he "never left Orkney" as has been held by journalists who used to think of him as living the exact same life as his crofter and fisherman characters. He eventually succeeded in correcting that presentation of him when he spoke of the six years he spent in Edinburgh - at Newbattle Abbey College and then at the University of Edinburgh - with great warmth. The discipline of study would surely open new horizons for him, and while enjoying the literary camaraderie of Edinburgh and the Rose Street pubs, he made many friends. But he said in a TV interview that he did no writing at that time.

When he came back to live beside his widowed mother, he stayed, only going back south as a visitor to see friends. Stromness was his home town, his hamnavoe. It is a jewel of a town, in a brilliant setting, with a miniature urban life of its own. Most of its inhabitants have neither boat nor croft, but there are hidden gardens, sheltered and very lovely, in among and between the stone houses and the twisting wynds and long flights of stone steps built into the steep slope of Brinkie's Brae. The children nowadays who swarm its long street after school are brightly dressed like children anywhere, effortlessly swearing as they go by, in that calm way children have, and always eating, out of bags of chips or packets of sweet stuff.

It is not essentially different from the street along which wee boys in George's schooldays ran off after school to play football or to watch the town's tradesmen at work. All the same, in readings of GMB's work, the sentimentality suggested especially in some radio productions which have the reader or actor using a sort of soft mock-Highland/ mock-Orcadian accent from nowhere strikes me as exaggerated and unfair. He was better served by the late John Broom's reading, both of serious work and some lighter items, like GMB's matter-of-fact account of how he made home-brew in giant plastic containers in his Mayburn Court kitchen, read laconically by John for a hilarious contribution to a Johnsmas Foy, one Saint Magnus Festival.

Of George Brown's plays, the one I remember as coming over on a high level was a production at the Orkney Arts Theatre in the early seventies, directed by an SCDA adjudicator, of "Jock and Blind Mary", with Walter Leask playing Jock and Queenie Campbell as Mary. I never knew George well, but on meeting him by chance in the butcher/greengrocer's shop, or at events in the Pier Gallery, he was always very affable, and now he is gone he will be a miss.

Cartoons by "Spike". Reproduced with the permission of the family.

"A Thread Too Bright for the Eye" an appreciation of George Mackay Brown

Gerry Cambridge

I first met George in the summer of 1985. I was young, had been writing poetry for a year or two, and was in the islands writing a travelogue for English magazine. I had sent George a letter saying I hoped we could meet. About a week later, his reply - the first of many, all penned in his neat, careful script - said he'd be pleased to. He hoped the weather would be decent for me: "A bit of sun and wind, even the occasional shower, makes Orkney look beautiful...."

Our first meeting wasn't prearranged. With the brashness of youth, and prompted by John Barleycorn, I knocked on the door of his council house one July evening. He'd have been entitled to refuse to see me, yet he ushered me in. I stayed half an hour. When he heard I wrote poetry - how often he must have heard that with a sinking of the heart! - he said, "Keep your manuscripts, Gerry. Keep them in a box under your bed so when the buyer of manuscripts comes round you can sell them to him."

"I doubt if I'll ever reach that stage, George."

"You mustn't throw anything out, anyway."

Our second meeting, several days later, was in the bar of the Royal Hotel in Stromness. *Smoke Gets In Your Eyes* was playing on the juke box. George crooned and caterwauled along with it in the lulls in the conversation.

"You wouldn't make much of a singer, George," I said. "It's as well you're a poet."

He was taller than one expected, and of slight build. What struck me most on first meeting him were his features. He had an extraordinarily expressive face, very distinctive, with a strong protruding chin which he could - it seemed - thrust out this way and that at will; his cheekbones were very marked, high, with the skin taut over them, giving his face a noticeable leanness, the whole topped by a lavish cloud of grey-white hair. When he made some remark, he would look at you sidelong, a gleam in his blue eyes, observing your reaction.

We talked about letter writing. I said I wrote letters carefully, almost like an article or a poem.

"That's probably because you're a nice human being," said the friend accompanying him, with exasperated affection. "Not like George. George just churns them out like a computer."

"Oh yes," said George, equably. "I can switch from poems to short stories or letters at the drop of a hat. That's no bother."

"But your letters are so *cold*," said his friend. "As if they'd been written by a machine. What about if someone was really sick and needed one of your letters to help them?"

"They'd be in a poor way indeed," he replied, "if that were so."

He had a great sense of the ridiculous, a gift for mimicry, a sharp satirical eye. Speaking of one visiting poet, he said, "He was almost neurotic, Gerry. And quite vain. Going past a window, he'd check his appearance in it." And he went through the motions of smoothing back his hair with elaborate slowness and gravity, and adjusted his tie with his chin thrust proudly out. His face was so distinctive already that this was hilarious.

I told him I'd met a local character and drank a few pints with him.

"Be careful around him," he said.

"Why, is he violent in drink?"

"Quite violent and also religious," he said. "He tries to convert you. And if that doesn't work he hits you - punches you into the kingdom of heaven."

When I returned to the mainland, my correspondence with George over the following winter helped give me a sense of connection with the wider world of poetry. Thereafter, into the early 90s, half a dozen times a year or so I would send him batches of poems; back would come the responses - a mix of encouragement, criticism and advice. It was George who confirmed me in the idea of an apprenticeship in poetry. In one early letter he wrote:

> The important thing, I think, is: poetry must have structure. It is not to be confined, it is to be forced to seek resources in language, to mine deep for the right word and phrase that yet chime in felicitously with the rest. Nowadays - alas - verse looks too easy. I think any new poet should spend a year at least learning the traditional forms of English prosody. After that, he should see his way clear.

He was a terse, pertinent, and often wry correspondent. In one letter he mentioned he was making some recordings for the local archives. "The assistant archivist," he wrote, "is a sweet beautiful young woman and so maybe I'll recite and chant better than if they sent a severe, strict lady...". He wrote to me in January last year:

> I shuffle around, a poor old creature, since winter began. I put nose out of door, an icicle depends from it; then I retire snuffling to the warmth of the fire. If only a few poems and stories sang out of the bare branches, I'd be thankful. But nothing. I had a go at a poem last week - it gave two chirps and thudded on the ground.

Less than a year after our first meeting, back in Orkney for a week in May, I visited him for tea several times in the afternoons at his council house, which with a private garage below it, was raised one floor up, with a seaward window, and redolent of the sea. I remember these as occasions of lyrical delicacy, George pouring tea from a china teapot into china cups with saucers, and sitting with his slim hands in his lap in the little light-filled room, or pushing back a wing of hair that flopped over his brow, or occasionally humming in the silences, his glance darting about the room before meeting your eyes an instant, then glancing away again. "You look a bit like Van Gogh, Gerry," he once said.

"You look a bit like George Mackay Brown, George," I said, and we laughed.

One spoke about poetry with him quite tentatively, as if trying to get a butterfly to land on a fingertip. About his own poetry he said little, and it wasn't done to show him any of your own work in person.

In good weather, you could often find him at the pierhead getting a blink of sun, sometimes with other locals. I once introduced myself to him there, and he made a space for me on the bench. As I sat down, the local he'd been speaking with rose. "Well George," he pronounced, "I don't think I'd like to meet anither author. What's your name sir? - George? - Gerry? - I'd better away, and keep me stories to mesel."

George was possibly the least intimidating author one could meet. He would float a feather of a question in the air about some book or author, and if you didn't grasp it, let it float off, and turn to other topics. I felt that he always kept a sound perspective on the difference between art's struggle to express difficult truths, and reputation. I visited him once soon after he'd been awarded some honorary degree or other. "It's ... very nice of them, Gerry," was all he said, with a smile. I felt he was as happy blethering to the locals - to whom he was plain George Brown - as with other writers, famous or otherwise. Perhaps he knew instinctively that respectableness or any form of pretension may be, at root, the enemy of poetry, which comes from the edge, and from what is fundamental in us: "I will sing you the music of the beggarman," as Yeats wrote: "Homer's music." George was confident in his art, yet personally modest. Perhaps it was to avoid the dangers - and sometimes the necessities - of pretentiousness that he insisted on the idea of poetry as craft, as not necessarily more praiseworthy than other trades. Once, when we talked about the younger writers who had adopted Stromness, he joked: "I'll be out of business if this goes on, Gerry. I'll have to put the shutters up."

En route to some of the smaller islands, I'd always visit George when passing through Stromness. He seemed a centre for the town. He appeared intrigued and amused at the idea of my going out to stay for the summers on some of the remoter islands to write, as I did at the end of the eighties, exchanging labour at a crofter's haywork for free lodging in an old butt and ben without plumbing or electric. "You'll still be there at 85, Gerry," he quipped, "writing your own version of *The Prelude*." Or he'd advise: "Work for two or three hours a day, like a sentry on duty. Then let the wind and sea-sounds wash over you. So says this ancient bard."

What one takes from George's example as a writer is the desire to go one's own way, irrespective of literary fashions. Like all authentic artists, he tried to take, I believe, "the long view", both of his own work and that of others. "Most contemporary verse," he once commented to me, "would be better lighting the fire with."

When the great American poet Robinson Jeffers, whose work George admired, first moved to the coast of California where his finest poems are set, he observed that it was the constancies of human existence which provided the soundest ground for durable poetry. While George's later work became more lyrical and mystical, in some of the earlier work there is an implied desire that art be functional, linked to the basic rituals of human existence. So Arnor the poet, at the end of "The Five Voyages of Arnor", requests of Erling Saltfingers, after his, Arnor's death:

drop my harp
through a green wave, off Yesnaby,
next time you row to the lobsters.

George created the taste, as Eliot said poets had to, by which he would be appreciated. His adopted Catholicism informed some of his verse; but one feels that the strength in his poetry doesn't lie in such devotional pieces. Blake said that Milton was a true poet, the devil got the best part. But to me, George's finest poems refuse, or don't consider, the consolation of faith. I wrote to him when his own most recent selection of *The Selected Poems* appeared, quizzing him about some of the omissions, such as "The Funeral of Ally Flett". It contains lines strong by any standard:

Because his dance was gathered now
And parish feet
Went blundering their separate roads
After the plough
And after net and peat and harvest loads
Yet from the cradle
Their fated steps with a fixed passion beat,
Tammas brought his Swedish fiddle.

He made no response as to why he'd omitted it, but one wondered if, as with Wordsworth's re-writing of *The Prelude* in old age, it had to do with the older man's correction of his daemon. The poem celebrates the round of death and birth, but without religious consolation. Other striking omissions were pieces such as "Ikey on the People of Hellya", the beautiful love poem, "Country Girl", and that marvellous lyric, "Shroud". From the forthrightness of its opening statement, "Seven threads make the shroud", the poem lists those threads by colour - "a blue fish thread", a green corn thread", and so on, finishing with "a thread too bright for the eye". A close reading shows that only "the white thread" and "the black thread" are referred to by the definite article, as if, perhaps, the qualities they symbolise are held to go beyond the temporal. The poem unobtrusively sets up, within its nine lines, a shimmer of suggestive energies.

George seemed to have little time for confessionalism or personal revelation in poetry. As an environment, the Orkneys don't encourage introspection. Anyone who has spent time on one of the smaller islands knows how the experience throws you back on your own resources. In practical matters, for instance, tradesmen cannot be called out easily. The resourceful islander learns to make and do. Externals, the importance of action as opposed to being, are paramount. Perhaps this accounts for

George's occasional dismissal of confessional poetry - for, after all, one only has time for such concentration on the self when the other aspects of existence have been solved. He once said to me, perhaps not entirely jokily, that he was a "cradle Calvinist". Much of his own poetry is a celebration of hard externals. A poem such as "Beachcomber", for example, which uses his familiar motif of the number 7, and which George perhaps noticed in a Hardy poem (where the latter uses the seven days of the week to chart the progress of a love affair) is a startlingly original performance. There is little of Frost's "inner weather" here, except as imposed from without by the environment. The stanzas sit on the page like islands, their nouns and verbs as strong and definite as some inhabitants of the Orkneys:

Monday I found a boot -
Rust and salt leather.
I gave it back to the sea, to dance in.

George's use of language is unique - derived from a mix of Anglo-Saxon (which he told me he particularly enjoyed studying at university) and latinate diction, from his fondness for Hopkins, and from the sharp, dryly-witty speech of the islands. Though he began writing in traditional forms and never entirely abandoned them, he developed his own style of free verse. I remember discovering a poem of his in (I think) *Scottish Poetry Nine*. Called "Trees", it is about a young girl visiting the city from Orkney. It has the opening confident flourish of a virtuoso:

A certain girl is out of the islands,
she with spillings of sunbright hair.

To my surprise, he thought nothing of this poem when I mentioned it.

And now there will be no more poems, letters, stories or novels, no more meetings, or goodbyes at his door, his eyes lit, his chin going this way and that, his face looking like it was two faces at once, one serious and the other, tussling with it below, laughing – kindly – as at some great joke. At his sunlit burial at Warbeth, below Stromness, with the blue-gray hills of Hoy epic across the sea, a breeze from off its miles lifting the hair of the mourners, nesting peewits and curloos trilled and swooped and display-flighted in the fields about the stones. George would have appreciated them. One remembers with gratitude his diamond gaiety, achieved at cost, but genuine:

The tall bright arch on the black cloud -
as the squall rushes the islands,

rattling the panes, grimacing women and men -
as the vast cloud speeds off over the sea,

fades; and the clear light blazes round.
So the seven hues die to the sun again.

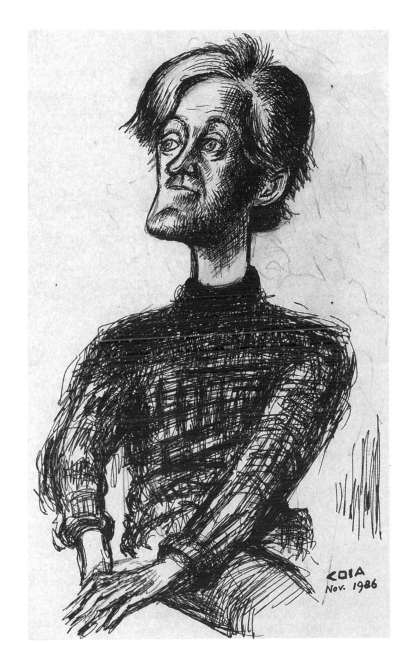

Illustration by Emilio Coia

Sam Gilliland

Canzone 3
(For GMB)

Our Norseman has gone and the islands mourn,
Viking Gods hear the dirge and the craped drum
Slowly tapping. His longboat glides on a misty swell
Upsurging that will take him on a journey well
Travelled, and by other warriors bourne
Into time's own dark ocean where the thrum
And lyre of bards bid others come;
Now, in that boundless, silent sleep,
Where the great dead in their vigil keep
Valhalla bright by that Northern star,
He'll travel well, and he'll travel far.

The Prostitute in Palma

You stand with your arms behind you,
Hands pressed against the church wall,
Seeking love in stones.
Old men come to you like new suns
Flushed with dawn, and your short pink
Skirt has no armour to repel them.
Crowds of people mill past like an unseeing
River, but they sway and undulate, leaving
A gap between you and them,
An unwritten charter where sweet flesh
Is sometimes seen as the sour wine
Of song.

Now and then a young man lingers,
And wistful eyes shake out your truth,
As if Orpheus laid bare your breasts
And kissed a naked winter onto lips
Made as brazen as a platinum moon.

Behind your cleaving glance
A child measures moments and
Green corn robs itself of gold.
Your withering began with the haste
Of blossoming womanhood seeking a
Way through a darkened labyrinth of
Quickening men and the mocking laughter
Of Gods tearing the wings off
A butterfly.

GACELA *of corrupted love*

Where long dead sorrows melted in my mouth,
And cherry nipples arched to a dappled sun
That fledged the marrow of my youth
Whose bridal song had just begun
To mock both the image and the bone.

Once laughter danced in every vein,
And immortal flesh, filled with love's desire,
Tore music from the body's pain
Birthing songs for Death's dark ear
From the throbbing drum of a quivering groin.

And the hollow history of a lover's seed,
Trembled in virgin joy with truthful need
Of the sensuous breast and naked thigh,
But the truth, in time, became a lie.

Olhos D'Agua

It's been three years since we
Sat on the beach at
Olhos D'Agua, sipping
Vinho verde and eating
Chicken piri piri with our
Fingers as wandering waves
Lapped at our feet
And salt stained our shoes.

Remember how, at night,
The lights on the prow
Of piraguas shone,
Glittering like eyes in the sea.
And how crickets sang ancient tunes
To the murmur of breakers
Caressing rocks along the bay
As lonely women, in sea-shell houses,
Watched for a flaming lamp.

In that soft flesh of evening
We loosed our thoughts to dreams
As we sipped and tasted
The salt-tanged air;
Hailing a mellowed sun
We kissed in sacred shadows
When we heard tomorrow's whisper
And the echo of yesterday.

O, that is my Iberia,
That part of Portugal
Spilling down to the sea
Where fishermen run out boats
As a shimmering moon
Heaves wide her net
From a glittering basilica of stars.

Kevin Williamson

The Poets Boarded The Ark

The poets came in two by two
Bukowski with his dogs
William Butler with his swans
Norman with his frogs.

Carlos Williams came with felines
Right paw, left paw, left paw, right
Larkin brought some dancing horses
Stepping gaily what a sight.

Milton slithered up the gangplank
Eating apples with the snakes
Morgan hissed just right behind him:
"Siesta time – let's take a break."

But last said Rabbie in a hurry
With forty ladies dressed up bright:
"To hell with cowering timorous beasties
I've bold ones here for every night!"

My Mind Is Like My Bed

always in a mess
never made up
but empty without you.

Epithalamium

She married him on the same day
I broke my nose against the jewelled
right fist of a scrumhalfbullneckdoorman
outside Europe's Premier Nightspot (Barnsley).

The twilightzonemaninblack had said:
"Now's your chance, mate. Got something to say?"
I should have obliged. Took up his offer.
Whatever it is you're supposed to do.

But she was a million miles away.
And I was no hoffmanfigurebedraggled.
For once, I stayed silent as an eclipse. Hurt.
Outside Europe's Premier Nightspot (Barnsley).

Tricky One

Just the other day
I was pondering
on the mysteries of life
as you do

wondering
what came first -
Tom Leonard
or Irn Bru?

Moving Statue
(Ben Bhraggie At Dusk)

It could be anything
the light on the hill.

The brightest firefly in the universe!

This hill with its gentle
slopes and its back

to the barren wasteland
of former havens.

Its sheep are like dandruff.

On a pedestal stands the duke
at the summit of his powers

casting his stony eye
to the north sea to his castle.

Dunrobin? Fuckin right he is.

Aye, it could be anything
the light on the hill.

A match struck? Dynamite?
Here's hoping.

Blades

Raymond Soltysek

So what the fuck am I doing here? Twelve years since I've been in this place and it's still too busy, too much noise and toilets that stink and hot water that you can't use because it would strip your skin off. You'd think they'd sort a water heating problem in twelve years. The people are still the same, girl students dressed in black and insurance salesmen in grey suits, even the same hairy oddballs, shepherds down from the isles who won't touch anything except Laphraoig.

It's not them who are the problem, though. It's you. I don't know you any more.

Good to see you, I say. We shake hands, old pals. *How's life?*

Fine, you say.

How many is it now?

Three. One of each.

Ha Ha.

Aye, Daniel's fourteen.

Is he? Fuck, time flies.

I stand with my hands stuffed in my pockets, juggling my unproductive nuts.

No, no children,
not married.
Got close with Anne, though,
lucky escape, eh?
I've never felt the need,
I'm too old now anyway,
thirty-seven,
can you imagine?

Only in situations like this do I make excuses. I am young. I feel as young as I did when we were a team, drinking a dozen Big Whitbreads on Friday nights during the brewery strikes and dancing together at the Savoy, me looking the biz in my greenstitch Wranglers and black velvet jacket but never getting a lumber because I didn't know how. Christ, I couldn't tell you that, going home and falling asleep with the headphones on, waking up to the record pop-pop-popping at the end of the track, ears roasting, while you were away with the blonde or the brunette or the redhead you'd picked up, French kissing and getting your hole. You and Tom and Andy. All of you. Got married to one of those sweet girls who said "Yes" when you asked them if they wanted a drink, sweating after Roxy Music's latest had brought you together. All of you. But you were the best. The luckiest.

No.

I feel younger. Time has served me well.

I look younger. Than you. Tom says so, sporting a creamy moustache of Guinness. *When are you going to grow old, ya bastard?* I boast about getting into thirty-inch waist jeans, not since the last year at Uni. Tom has thickened : so have you, I see, well fed prosperity under a lambswool sweater of grey and lemon diamonds. Mad Andy, still whippet, adrenaline consuming carbohydrates...

Listen, do you remember that gendarme,
tried to arrest Andy, threatened to shoot him with a fucking big gun but settled for kicking his arse for pissing up against the plate glass wall of a restaurant, fancy French diners open-mouthed, showing their half-chewed escargot. Andy ran off, legs flying, arms flying, dick flying, bellowing "poulet" over his shoulder at the gendarme. Lucky we met him on the way back from the campsite, red mist in his eyes, Swiss Army knife in his hand. He could have cut himself.

I remember that holiday. You and me sat on the boxy little beach at Dinard in the dark and drank duty-free Glenfiddich from the neck and talked a load of shite but it was magical.

It isn't mentioned.

I was the only one sensitive enough to get teenage clinical depression, and did you all suffer for it. Morbid angst of divorced parents and family secrets and insecurity and lack of self-esteem that had me screaming nightmares at three in the morning, saying nothing during whole evenings in the pub having been uncurled like a hedgehog from a corner of my bedroom, "Davie, Davie, what's up with you?" by wee sisters who didn't have a clue.

Sex was the real problem with me: you only mentioned it for a laugh. "Hey boys, do you think Davie's still a virgin?"

Of course I was.

Ha Ha.

I could have killed you, the ease, the chat, the simple invitation, the three month affair that ended, ended, ended, no pain. I fell, smitten, obsessed with girls who wouldn't fancy me in a million years, wrote "I love Elizabeth Mackie" in my diary over and over, took half a year to pluck up the courage to ask her out for a meal and felt the world cave in when she'd got herself a new boyfriend the night before, someone better than me, someone interesting.

You set your sights too high, you said.

Are you still setting your sights too high?

Naw,

I'm not interested.

I'm happy,

nice girlfriend,

no ties.

Oh, aye. You look over my shoulder, far off. *Hey boys, she's all right.* Not that far off.

She is. Blonde. Thirty-five-ish. Our tastes grow old with us. She wears a bit too much make-up and glittery earrings and is over-dressed for this pub - black velvet jackets must be making a come back. But she is. Definitely is. All right.

I imagine she sizes you up, measuring possibilities. She looks past me.

See, Davie, that was your problem. Like DB, she was always into big guys, the rugby players. She married Fergus, didn't she? You light a cigarette. *Or Lorna.*

Because she was yours. And I felt like hers, all for a touch on the arm, a word of kindness. You told me she talked of me. You shouldn't have said that. As far as I knew, she was the first who ever had. You gave me her 'phone number when you'd finished with her and watched the mayhem I caused, knowing I wouldn't have a thing to say, knowing I wouldn't know what to do. She must have found me torture, my face stuck in a plateful of pasta, my guts grinding for some inspiration and ending up arguing about religion. And blaming you, blameless you. If she goes to Hell, she'll probably spend eternity on that date with me. What a fucking mess I was. "You've got a lot of hang-ups, Davie," she said. Serves me right. She was My Best Friend's Girl.

Aye, you never really told me how you got on with her.
Fine,
but everything was too
complicated,
complex,
tense.
You know
how it is,
how everyone would have felt
on an eightsome.
Or on a foursome, just me and Lorna, and you and?
But I was grateful, you know, for What You Did.
Funny, I'd almost forgotten that, you say. *Long time ago. These things happen.*

Things happen. Lots of things happened. They had to, our team laying waste, hormone-charged weekends when myths were guaranteed. You know everything there was about me, and I wonder what you have done with all that information over the years. Perhaps the butt of nostalgic jokes, always my worst fear. I still avoid situations with the potential for ridicule, feigning headaches, keeping my profile low, so low it's positively subterranean.

Ha Ha.

Perhaps you sympathised over long dinners, you all, wives too, candles and best china and crudités followed by a wholesome pasta dish and Vienetta for pud. Or maybe it was your fondue period when Habitat was the place to be and you'd sit there and say, "Remember Davie, what a nice guy he was, shame about the…"

Face. The blonde's face swims into view, around Andy's shoulder. You have seen her coming, already prepared. *Do you have a light?* she says, and you half turn, cup your hands around hers to shield the flame and smile, establish complicity in the reprehensible habit, one to start off with. You are lost to us, Tom nudges, winks, and I think, Heck of a guy.

In the Griffin, all of nineteen, standing pishing pure lager mob-handed on a Saturday night and that guy at the roller towel talked to you, older, perhaps mid-twenties. You spoke about the rugby, Scotland won and wasn't it a great game and he offered you a cigarette. Piling out, he followed us, sat perched pint in hand on a stool beside you, smiled at your profile and once, just once, patted your knee. You knew what was going on, could feel the thrill of the pick-up in him, and ignored it. Desperate, he was, and when I asked him to leave, he said, "You can have him," slammed his pint down so hard it spilled and soaked your cigarette packet, but still you didn't crack, and I sat there with my heart thumping and my knees shaking as the door swung back heavy on those big brass hinges. We all went to The Penthouse, a dive full of dogs, you said, and you lumbered that wee cutter fae Pertick with the spots and the black boob tube. What's a cutter, you asked us.

I didn't know.

The blonde detaches herself, her cigarette already half smoked. You return, smile, *All right, boys?* and soul of discretion, talk of golf. Tom's a club championship man, won it two years ago, in the top ten for the last six, and you whistle low, can't get your handicap down past ten, and Andy, thrashing the ball round the course with his animal energy, will never see the right side of ninety-five. I have a set of clubs at home, growing old at the back of a cupboard, hardly swung since I bought them with my first pay cheque. No-one to show me the ropes, I tell myself.

I write stories,
and there is a silence, gob-smacked, not much of a social life there Andy supposes, and you draw on your cigarette and mention work. You are all engineers.

The roads you have planned!
The bridges you have built!
The boilers you have stoked!

Do you remember we shared a bed once, pissed at Tom's party, dossing down on a mattress slung slanted on the back room floor, cot wedged in the corner, billowing out gentle wafts of baby smell, talc and bile and God knows what? I didn't know then. You would now. You smacked your lips all night as you slept, woke me up to the room circling but never seeming to go anywhere, like a spirit level bubble. I crawled to the toilet and was sick, long hard sick that burned my throat but I felt better and managed back on my feet and found some girl had crept in beside you, one you had been chatting up all night and who I thought had left. She slung her arm over your shoulders, and the light outside was coming up and I looked at her dark eyes and she went "Sshh" and pulled the blankets open behind her. I sagged into the bed and she moved closer to you so that our skin wouldn't brush, and I lay awake till seven, the back of my head, my shoulder blades, my spine, my buttocks and thighs and calves and heels tingling at the untouch of her, then fell asleep and when I woke you weren't there. You never mentioned her.

Neither did I.

But I asked where you'd gone. Tom's wife smiled and gave me breakfast and told me not to worry, I didn't need you, I wasn't married to you even though we acted like it sometimes. And why aren't you going out with someone, she asked, you're a good-looking guy. She didn't like to see me in your shadow, she said, and anything could happen, there was so much tension between us. I cringed, wanted away from the child in the high chair by the breakfast table and the sun streaming in the window right into my eyes so that I couldn't read her face, not that I would have understood the message anyway. Then Tom came back from getting the Sunday papers and the conversation was dropped and I was relieved, though I spent the next week sleepless thinking about Tom's wife and the girl in the bed and wanked myself stupid.

In the mirror behind you, the blonde looks over. She has a friend, tall, brown haired, a nose slightly hooked but beggars can't be and a possibility flashes through my head. I focus on your reflection, notice your crown, thinning, and dismiss the prospect.

You shuffle, impatient, drain your glass and belch softly. It's time for us to go. We drag coats on, jostle to the door, open to the cool night air, and stand just outside, a light drizzle freshening my face as we say our goodbyes.

Well, lads, good seeing you again, you say.

Andy is overcome, *it's been too long boys, what about same day next month?* Tom agrees, *we were a team,* really close, so important to keep in touch with each other, with the past.

I put my past to the test, I have grown up now, I can cut the crap.

D'you know, in lots of ways we were like lovers.

Behind you, in the light of the pub, it seems there is a wall of faces. One brick in it moves, the blonde gathering up her handbag and kissing her friend, goodbye, on the cheek.

You look back at me, peering bland as pork through cigarette smoke. *Maybe you were,* those clipped tones, exasperation. *I wasn't.*

Taming the Scots

Malcolm Lobban

So, ye think the Scots are hard done by wi the Tories? Well, let me jist tell ye somethin, the rot set intae this country o oors a long while afore even Maggie Thatcher came oan scene. As a metter o fact, while Ah think o it, it wis anither wummin ca'd Maggie who helped tae heid the ba intae the Scottish goalmooth, as it were. . . an she wis English as well.

Ah suppose it aa began as faur back as the year Ten Thirty. There wis the king fund lyin deid ootside a smithy's bothy near Elgin. His name wis Dunky, although some folk ca'd him Duncan the Gracious. Ah think this must've been because he didnae use bad sweary words, an aye said "pardon" everytime he riftit! Anyhow, the poor bugger seems tae hiv been murdert.

Naebody knows why he wis at Elgin in the first place, 'cause it didnae even hiv a decent fitba team in they days. But the polis suspectit that Dunky's cousin — a bloke ca'd Macbeth — had a haun in it.

Of coorse, the media got it aa wrang as usual. They tried tae pit the blame oan Macbeth's wife, a wee wummin ca'd Gruoch. They tried tae say that she egged her man oan, in the hope that he wid get promotion by gettin rid o poor auld Dunky.

As it turned oot, they had nae sooner clapped doon the durt oan Dunky's grave when the bold Macbeth, who up tae this time had been nothin mair than a regional councillor in Moray, took owre the family business, Crown Enterprises plc. In fact, he actually became king o the castle, as it were, fur the next sixteen years, until finally he wis threatened wi a takeowre fae south o the Border.

The challenge came fae the late King Dunky's eldest son, a punter ca'd Malky Bigheid. Some say he got his nickname efter he became a heid bummer in later life. But Ah've also heard tell that it wis because o the size o his napper, an that he could easily cairry a stane o tatties in his bunnet.

Malky Bigheid wis only nine when his faither was killt, so he wis sent doon tae stay wi freens o the family in South Britain — that's whaur England is noo. He went tae school there an soon learnt the ways o the native Anglefolk.

By the time he wis auld enough, and had earnt himsel A-levels in art o serfbashin, he decidit tae come hame again an try fur his late faither's auld job – or at least mibbe a gaffer's job in the family business. But it seems his uncle Macbeth wisnae playin that gemme, an he mair or less telt Malky tae go forth an try some ither entrepreneurial agency, like the Jobcentre, or mibbe jine the Knight's Templars or, better still, the Freemasons. At any rate, it seemed there wis nae chance that Malky wid get ane fit in the door in Scotland.

Of coorse Malky tried tae reason wi his uncle Mac. He even resortit tae sleekit threats, like tellin him that, if he didnae let him intae the business, the day wid come when a bauldy-heidit Englishman ca'd Wullie Shakespeare wid ane day make his name mud fae ane end o Britain tae the ither!

This must hiv finally rattled the teuchter king, who seems tae hiv lost the heid completely an ca'd oot his sodgers fur war. Malky, meanwhile, wis ready fur him an had gethert up a wheen o Geordies an ither assortit Sasunnachs, got them fu wi Newcastle broon ale, an marched north.

Baith armies met near a wee place ca'd Lumphanan in Grampian Region, whaur they knocked hell oot o ane anither. Ah think this wis the only hame gemme that Macbeth ever lost, fur he got killt, an the bold Malky Bigheid wis hame fur good.

Efter aa this, things kinda settlet doon fine fur a wee while in Scotland. But, aroon Ten Sixty-Six, things were no sae good owre the Border. It seems a big gang o neds – probably fu o Bordeaux wine – came owre oan the ferry fae Normandy an raidit the wee seaside toun o Hastings. They were led by a punter ca'd Wullie the Conqueror, an the raid caused great panic among the natives – Ah suppose ye could say it wis definitely "ane in the eye" fur their leader King Harold, who wis killt in the melee!

This Wullie the Conqueror took owre England. Ah suppose he wis yer orginal Tory, fur his heid wis fu o fancy ideas aboot how tae run the country. An like the Tory clowns we're lumbert wi the day, he wis aa fur free trade – but only if him an his sidekicks got the maist oot o it. This led tae economic recession an mass unemployment among the Anglefolk, who didna even hiv time tae organise trade unions, an great misery swept owre the land.

The new King Wullie wis also intae Privatisation in a big way. He flung aa the Anglefolk oot o their communal lands and tenements then replaced them wi his ain card-cairryin crawlers an arse-lickers. They came tae be ca'd earls, barons and knights.

The name of the gemme wis, if ye didnae bow the heid an kiss Wullie's haun – or mibbe some ither part o his anatomy – ye didnae get yer land back, nor a wee bit parchment tae tell folk that ye were ane o King Wullie's gang! Actually, he wis mibbe the first tae invent quangos, which he soon spread aa owre the country – but he ca'd them baronies an burghs!

The poor Anglefolk wur obliged tae pledge themsels tae their new heidyin or emigrate. Many o them turnt their attention tae Dunfermline (nothin tae dae wi the Buildin society o that name), this was whaur oor ain King Malky Bigheid's main office wis at that time. The poor refugees were lookin fur asylum – an they picked the right ane, Ah can tell ye!

Malky Bigheid, meanwhile, wis busy brushin up oan his Gaelic an gein it big licks wi the hee-do-rum-haws, an aa that. Bein sae long away in England, his membership o An Comunn Gaidhlig had lapsed. But he aye waantit tae know whit aa his Heilan punters were greetin aboot, afore he telt them tae get stuffed. But bein the big glaikit eedjit that he wis, he meanwhile let in aa the Anglefolk that came chappin at his door.

Amang the new white settlers wis a man ca'd Edgar, who wis the heir tae the late King Harold. He asked Malky if he could mibbe find him a job in the Scottish government — as long as it wisnae anythin tae dae wi the Ministry o Defence, since his ain track record, like that o King Harold, wisnae very good. Nevertheless, he haundit owre his CV tae Malky an said he wid consider ony job. . . as long as it involved tellin ither folk whit tae dae!

The bold Malky, meanwhile, wis itherwise busy eyein up a tidy wee bit o stuff who wis staunin kinda in the backgroon. This wis Edgar's wee sister Maggie — a real doll— an this is the wummin tae watch!

Malky's brain wis taen owre completely, an also workin overtime tryin tae figure oot the best way fur him tae get aff wi Maggie. . . mibbe even a durty weekend in his caravan at Arbroath. But she wis no the wummin fur that carry oan. She wis too fly fur his uncouth patter, an wisnae fur touchin even the toorie oan his tartan bunnet. No, at least, until she got the nod fae the Bishop of Rome. . . an a fair-sized daud o the precious yella metal oan her dainty wee digit!

So, Malky Bigheid, besottit an beside himsel wi lust, gied owre his heart an heritage by finally gettin merrit tae Princess Maggie. Thus, whilst the trumpets hailed the nuptial vows, they forby heralded the beginnin o the end fur Celtic Scotland – an Parkheid had nothin tae dae wi it. Queen Maggie, forby takin owre the keys o the hoose, taen owre maist of the business as well.

It wis her who showed King Malky how tae use a knife an fork – an she even made him change his Y-fronts mair than once a month. No only that, but in atween the occasional sair heids at bedtime, she did manage tae gie him eight weans. She also encouraged mair o her ain Anglefolk tae come tae Scotland – they aa thought it wis a rerr place tae open up B-an-B hooses in touns as faur apart as Saltcoats an Portobello.

Queen Maggie wisnae awfie fond o oor staple diet. She didnae like purritch, haggis, clootic dumplins, cauld pies or fried breid. She startit tae import her ain luxury things fae England an the Common Market area. In nae time at aa, King Malky wis feastin oan fish an chips wi mushy peas, or mibbe tripe an ingans done wi mulk. Then there wis pan-breid fur the pieces, an mibbe the odd toastit muffin. Oot went the pints o heavy bevvy an the wee goldies, an in came the stem-glesses o Rid Biddy – or mibbe a cheekie wee Buckfast, noo an then! Aye, it wis aa changed days in Scotland, an nae mistake.

Maggie wisnae aa that keen oan how ordinary punters went aboot things in their everyday lives. She immediately fell oot wi the auld Celtic kirk, then brought in ane o her ain fae Rome. Besides aa this, she wis aye conscious o her ain personal appearance in public – especially whaur the media wis concernt. She wis awfy careful aye tae keep ane or two poor folk handy, so that when the reporters came aroon they wid see her either shovin watter biscuits intae wee weans' mooths, or mair likely she'd be gein some poor leper a pedicure. In them days there wisnae any folk wi AIDS tae be seen shakin hauns wi!

Aa this cairry oan, alang wi her part-time agency work fur the Pope, kept Maggie quite busy. But Ah've aye hid a strong notion that she wis mibbe mair concernt owre her ain salvation, than the poor, torn-arsed wee sowls she kept hingin roon her midden. She mibbe saw her charity work as some kind o celestial insurance policy fur her ain redemption. If it wis, then it seems tae hiv worked in her favour. . . nothin as ordinary as a seat in the Hoose o Lairds fur this Maggie, naw indeed. . . the holies o the day made her a saint, nae less!

Apart fae this, Queen Maggie seems tae hiv kept her man happy wi himsel, an aye made sure he hid oan his best armour when he went oot tae battle wi King Wullie doon south. Owre an above, she aye made sure that he hid plenty nice wee cucumber sannies in his sporran.

Malky Bigheid, meanwhile, wis gainfully employed, either tryin tae create boundary changes, or mair likely jist makin a bliddy nuisance o himsel among the new Norman yuppies in England. In fact, everytime him an his cronies left England, King Wullie wid discover things missin. . . like coos oot o the fields. . . an lead aff the kirk roofs.

Mind you, there wis a couple o times when Wullie got so pissed aff that he actually tried tae invade Scotland. On the first attempt, him an his two boys Boab an Bill brought an army as faur up as Abernethy. But they turned hame again – some say wi a cairt load o biscuits! Oan the secont attempt, they only got a faur as Falkirk. But the place must hiv been shut that day – mibbe it wis a Wednesday efternin. Anyhow, they turnt back, an oan the way hame, they built Newcastle and Carlisle as a kind o deterrent tae keep oot the Jocks – this wis long afore they built Wembley fitba park.

An aa the while the Anglefolk were still comin intae Scotland in their droves. At ane point even King Malky Bigheid wis getting a wee bit cheesed aff wi it. Mibbe he wis findin it mair difficult tae get a gemme o gowff in St. Andrews. The main problem wis, that whenever an Angleperson died in Scotland, anither hunder o them came tae the bliddy funeral an damn the ane that wid go back hame!

So, there ye hiv it. That's how poor auld Scotland came tae be "civilised." Oor country wis never ever completely conquert by foreign sodgers – no even the bliddy Romans could manage that. Mind you, fur an awfy long time there wisnae a helluva lot worth conquerin – no until we discovert ile aff Aberdeen, an that.

Naw, the plain truth is, the Normans didnae hiv tae invade us wi force. Oor ain stupit heid-bummers invitit them in, an it wis nae time at aa afore they took owre – an their descendants hiv been tellin us whit tae dae eversince. An that's how the maist o us Scots aa speak every bit as good English is whit they dae themsels!

If whaever reads this wee story should somehow fund certain similarities wi whit's happenin in modern Scotland, then it only goes tae show jist how how much we hivnae learnt fae oor past mistakes.

Scots hiv gein the world a helluva lot, born oot o their native genius an ingenuity. But, ye know, Ah sometimes think oor greatest talent is for scorin goals through oor ain goalmooth!

Illustration by Mary Gibons

Mary Jameson

Thinking of Emigrating

I have seen enough of Scotland,
    of sad dark hills, glens of sheep and stones,
    rock and rain and fretting seas,
    dour wind-tormented little towns.
I'd rather be where the sun bakes daily
    and sky is blue habitually
    Warm – I would be warm,
    in shadows which are smiling.

This barren Scotland breaks my heart –
    that accidental noble grace
    shows like some old wanton's proud, virgin heart
    brimming to the eyes when least aware.
She has been sold, and sold again, robbed
    but forgets her birthright, only in her dreams.

So, exiled I shall fancy
    this Scotland, unslaved, her own, uncorrupt.
    Drink whisky under hot skies and dream
    of home
    when work is done and day melts into dusk.
Sweet nightmares of a bitter land,
    a bitterness I shall forget,
    and leave behind in the sediment
    the peat Scotland is rooted in.
    There now grow little plastic flowers,
    smug flowers of greed, saccharine complaisancy
    and pawky saleable wit –
    Scotchness... "romance and charm";
    to entice foreign grabbers –
    creeping jenny, penny-come-quickly, yelly skelly,
    love-in-idleness, dead man's flourish
And that thistle, emblem of our race...
"Come wha's fer meddlin wi me?"

Oh what a garland for a hearse
    What flourish from what bitter earth!
    blood-nourished, salt with tears.
Yes I have seen enough, and felt enough
    the humiliation and sorrow
    of those dark haunted, empty glens,
    the scrap and filth of the grim towns
    where men are scrap and children want.

I know the heather beauty sold,
    the lochs and hills made rich men's play places,
    where soft-bellied robbers of the modern age
    play cruel and expensive games
but for the people there's a sign: "Keep Out"

I shall not think of the Scottish child in the foul close,
    nor the robber barons and their ill-got oil.
I shall not think of the pulp forests, bed and breakfasts,
    kilted soldiers, mercenary sons,
    kissing their wives and going far away
    to kill for masters they never saw.
    I shall not think of the empire that has hired our lives
    for London City and the stocks and shares.

But I shall dream of curled bracken in the gentle rain
    freckled children dabbling in a burn,
    the curlew's call at evening, and of skies
    dappled ceaselessly with blue and cloud
and a wind that smells of honey and of moss.

As I grow old and boring I shall lose
    this bitterness that eats into my bones
I shall never return, but build a lovely home
    of fond scraps... and dream of it. And dream
    till I am dead, and all dreams end?

Kevin MacNeil

Spring

Spring does not belong to the ordinary
senses. Watch how shadows deepen
and revive in the swooning sun.
(Their black glow is the quease and seethe
of jealousies I have known.)

Flowers settle, bees bubble with life,
miniatures of colourful lust.
(So, too, the dawn I arose by
my impossible love's side.)

Winter's bone-and-ice trees breathe light.
(They are buddhists rooted
in the warm flesh of fact.)

How this universe, the dharma wheel, turns
to a woman's most intimate gesture!

  (And how afterwards summer appeared
to astound us with its ordinariness.)

Fiach

Ged a tha iomadh bliadhna air a dhol seachad
bhon' thaisdeal naoi mìosan agam nad' bhroinn,
tha am fiach agam ort fhathast cho farsuing ris an fhàire,
thusa a bhitheas a' cur eagal orm le dragh is ròpan is gaol.

Ràinig na tuinn thu, dh'fhàisg iad thu, chum iad thu, lìon iad thu,
mus do leum an stoirm suas mar uilebheist bhon' àird-deas
Lìon na tuinn thu le pian, tonn an dèidh tuinn làn
le sàl do-fhaicsinneach, mol maolaich, gainmheach gharbh, dòmblas
dèisinneach.

'S cha chreid mi ach gur e mi-fhìn a chuir snàim air an ròpa.
Dh'fhan thusa cho trom ris an fhìrinn air an tràigh,
a' laighe sìos nad' throm-lighe shamhach fhèin,
's an làn-mara ag èirich mu do chuairt, searbh, fuar, neo-thruacanta.

Ged a tha mi a' feitheamh nise man seann dia, cogaiseach, iomallach,
neo-chomasach, chanainns' le cinnt gum bith thu ceart gu leòr.
Sàbhalaidh an dìoghaltas neònach seo thu, chì thu làithean ùra,
is bith thu beò (tha mi 'n dòchas) fhad 's a bhitheas seòladair na h-
inntinn seo beò.

Debt

*Though many years have passed since my nine-month voyage in you, my
debt to you is till as wide as the horizon, you who scare me with worry
and ropes and love. The waves reached you, they pinched you, they kept
you, they filled you, before the storm sprang up like a beast from the
south. The waves filled you with pain, wave after wave filled with
invisible brine, blunt shingle, rough sand, nauseous bile.
I believe nothing but that it was myself who put a knot in the rope. You
waited as heavy as the truth on the shore, lying down in your own silent
nightmare, the ride rising about you bitter, cold, relentless.
Though I am waiting now like an ancient god, remorseful, remote,
impotent, I would say with certainty that you will be all right. This weird
punishment will save you, you will see new days, and you will be alive (I
hope) as long as this sailor of the mind is alive.*

a red flower

a red flower
bows behind the tree,
flush of a lost girl's cheek

lost loch floating

lost loch floating
behind the mist
summer
is over.

quiet leaves

quiet leaves
floating against the snow
but slowly

each
one becomes
a hug you denied

Paul J Harrington

In Glasgow University

I pace the ancient Quad at lunchtime
under a coolness accumulated over centuries
by thick stone. The tower's bell
peals out the hour, late. Oak doors creak
in a monastery of sound –
the hush of dusty tomes resounds.
Head down professors traverse grass cubes
analysing Proust in their shoes;
and autumnal trees stand deep in leaves
strewn like texts cast off around the desk
of hunched, half–mad genius. I love this hushed place
where the outside world is muffled by paper,
by rows of spined seasons thickening the walls;
where holistic systems are unperturbed
by the freshers' dimpled dissent over details –
how does the scheme accommodate ripped jeans?
As the God shaped hole in the ozone gets bigger
books, brushed with the wish for a truant Christ,
reveal, like magical palimpsests, literature's ink
as the host of words holy beyond themselves.

Waking in Spring

The milkman's milk white knuckles clink
cream topped bottles on the concrete.
They chink to his whistle's lower key.
Up invisible in tree tops
birds pinprick the sky with twitters
as the milkfloat's tinkling thrum
adds to the chorus with its crates. It is spring.

Blue sky fries sun sunny side up.
And in kitchens early risers
wait for toast's renunciation
of its soft spongy status as bread,
its heedless leap from the heatclamps.
That's the effect of spring on wheat.
That's how you ought to meet the day.

But I prefer to lie in bed
blowing smokeballs to the ceiling
where they linger like giant ghosts' tears.
The day's first fag tastes sweet
in spite of bronchial rumours
and the sun nursing the room
coughmixture through the curtains,

a golden dose of glittering dust.
Peace seems to have settled here.
The clock has abandoned its second tick
for the pure moving silence of the big hands.
The downy is moulded around me
like earth around a bulb in a pot.
And the first bee of the season

is bumbling against the window
the summer's first bullet,
half dazed and yellow-black
shot across the bows of spring.
Life has acquired the good-looks
of flowers making their bid
to fill his empty pollen basket.

But it can't last: clouds are scooting
across the sky, frying bacon wafts
to the sound of butter sizzle,
a car backfires in the street.
And here comes the cat, a whiskered
purr-bundle licking its chops,
padding across the room to wake me.

For the Record

Marion Arnott

I grew up with stories about Samson the Israelite. My mother used to threaten that Samson would come and carry me off if I didn't eat up all my vegetables, or stop pulling the curling rags out of my hair and disgracing the family by going about with it poker straight. Even then, hardly more than a boy as he was, he was famous for terror.

Over the years, no one ever thwarted him. It seems his mother had a vision when he was born, and she brought him up to believe that he was so special that the normal rules did not apply to him. We all had to live with the consequences of that idea as he grew from just plain wilful to nightmarish. Everyone knows the stories. He burned animals alive, committed criminal arson, and crowned his career with the mass murder of one thousand Philistines with the jawbone of an ass of all things. And don't ask how he got hold of the jawbone, it's too gross for words.

He escaped punishment for all these horrors because he had worked out all the socially acceptable reasons for mayhem and murder: you know, patriotism, religion, and provocation by the female of the species. Samson claimed to be motivated by all three, which meant he could get away with just about anything. Credit where credit is due, he had a real genius for PR work.

You see, it wasn't what Samson did that mattered, it was how he told it. Murder, the Philistines said. Nothing of the kind, Samson said. He had been seized by the spirit of the Lord to smite all those Philistines. (For the record, he was resisting arrest on a charge of arson at the time). Arson? Nonsense, he said. There was a treacherous female at the bottom of that business, and all right, he'd been out of order but everybody knows how women can drive a man to distraction, and in the end he'd been forced to defend his personal honour. (What actually happened was that on his wedding day, he quarrelled with his in-laws after they won a silly guessing game. He went off in a huff to sulk in a cave for a few weeks, and when he came back ready to forgive everybody's unreasonable behaviour, he found that his bride, a lass of spirit, had upped and married someone with a sense of humour. Naturally, Samson went out and burned that year's harvest, along with three hundred jackals tied tail to tail, just to prove that he could be as funny as the next man).

After he burned the crops, many died of hunger, particularly old people and babies. The Philistines took exception to this, and that was when they tried to arrest him. He smote the militia, every man, hip and thigh with the jawbone. There was a tremendous fuss about that, even among the Israelites, but Samson appealed to their patriotism. After all, he had only killed Philistines who could not be counted as real people.

All that patriotism, spirituality, and personal honour impressed the Israelites no end, and they appointed Samson a judge over Israel as a mark of esteem. The simple truth was that Samson had a lust for killing; it was his nature; believe me, I know.

As for me, I am the discreditable part of the Samson legend, and there is nothing interesting about me except the time I spent between the sheets with Samson. Leastways, the singers and storytellers can't wait to get to that bit. They tell how there was a woman of the Philistines who lived in a valley and her name was Delilah. The hero Samson fell in love with her and came to a tragic end. Anyone would think I sprang into existence thirty seconds before I met him, with no other purpose in life but to seduce and destroy. For the record, there was a bit more to it than that.

I grew up the youngest of five sisters and not pretty. By the time I was of marriageable age, my mother was in despair at my lack of prospects. I weighed ninety five pounds soaking wet, and years of curling rags had done nothing to improve my straight mousey hair. I had long given up the dream of blossoming into a Rose of Sharon – I know a lost cause when I see one – but my mother was a very determined woman. She sewed cotton pads inside the fronts of my dresses to give me some shape, squandered a fortune in incense at the shrine of the Good Goddess, and let it be known around town that my dowry was being tripled. Eventually, she came up with a bridegroom, much to the amusement of my more fortunate sisters.

My husband was Ashtorek, only son of a bankrupt baker, and he was jug-eared and freckled, with a sort of helpless look about him. He always smelled of vanilla from the bakery, and he wrote poems to the stars, which he worshipped. We were an odd looking couple, but I liked him for his gentle ways, and I was more than able to run the bakery and make it pay. We grew close, Ashtorek and I, as we sat on the flat roof of the bakery, stargazing while the loaves browned in the big ovens below. We had plans: for the bakery, for children, even for a little venture into the business of exporting star maps to Babylon. Ashtorek drew beautiful maps.

Our plans came to nothing. Ashtorek was one of the thousand Philistines called up to face Samson in his rage the year he burned the harvest, one of those our hero smote hip and thigh. Two days it took to find Ashtorek among the dead. It was cold and eerie up there on the moors, what with the night wind rustling the long grass and carrying the sound of the keening of the women for miles around. To this day, I can still smell the blood. He was on his back with his eyes wide open to the cool little stars above. Such a look he had, empty-eyed and bewildered, my Ashtorek who couldn't fight his way out of a paper bag.

There was no time for mourning, we were all too busy surviving. The harvest failed again because there were no men to sow or reap. The military counted their losses up on the moor and drew a line under the total, but I counted the losses in the faces which came into my shop, the faces of widows and orphans and young girls who had no men to marry. They came for food, their faces pinched and gaunt, some with the death marks already on them. I had little to give. Useless mouths, the military called them, and took what there was to feed the fighting men. Children cried with hunger, and their mothers starved themselves to feed them; old folk swallowed poison so there would be more food for their grandchildren.

It was the best who died.

Months passed and the fields were sown again. Times improved, as times will, but they were never the same. Too many were gone from us, and Samson was a power in the land, a hero celebrated in song and story. His legend turned out to be more dangerous than he was. A cult grew up around him among our boys since a boy will follow a winner after all. They wore lion skins like his, and kept their hair long and shaggy à la Samson, were heavily into body-building, and cultivated explosive bad temper and divine viciousness. They forgot their dead fathers cold in the ground – defeat was shame, and the Samsonites had no time for sickly sentiment. All that was good and kind and civilised in our boys rotted away like the corn in the fields.

And so we come to the interesting part of the story, the part where I commit sex. Samson had a sweet tooth, and my cakes and biscuits were famed. He often came to the bakery, and then more often, accompanied by his entourage, a mixture of rabid patriots, religious fanatics, and the merely cruel. At night when I went up on the flat roof to look at the stars, I often considered poisoning him, but I thought his magic would be too strong for something so obvious. The secret of his invincibility was a national preoccupation, and the city was full of soothsayers and prophets reading the entrails and casting the runes to find it out. No one but me thought of asking Samson himself.

Samson liked his bread baked with herbs in it, and it occurred to me that the secret of his strength might lie in a potion or a powder he took. I baked his bread myself, and recommended other ingredients. Did he know the Egyptians swore by sesame seeds to increase stamina? Or that the Babylonians fed their athletes on this, that, or the other thing? I forget all that I said, but my powers of invention were endless. We chatted cosily about proteins and carbohydrates and fats, and his biceps and triceps and pecs. It was tedious work, but Samson was thrilled to find a woman who could hold a decent conversation; that is, whenever he didn't find it irritating, and remembered he didn't like know-all women. I was playing a very dangerous game. His irritation might lead him to blurt out his secret, just to put me in my place; on the other hand, it might erupt into violence. Still, there are risks that have to be taken. I prayed to the Good Goddess and persevered.

I was so preoccupied with gauging his moods and walking softly, that I did not realise he was becoming romantically involved until he took to lugging sacks of flour around with much flexing of muscle and effortless ease. I was careful to be impressed. Soon I was his Squirrel and his Field Mouse, even his little De-Lily-Of-De-Valley. That was his notion of wit, but I persevered with that too. Harder to deal with was his wish to bare his soul to me. He told me once that muscle sounded like wet cloth tearing when it was being ripped apart. He enjoyed sharing those thoughts.

We spent many evenings in such talk, but I never took him up on the roof, not even on the hottest nights. He was still coy about his secret, but it was only a matter of time before his need to impress would overcome his caution. In the meantime, he impressed me in other ways. He used to hold those big hammy hands of his before my eyes and say, "These hands are trained to kill", and tell me the story of the jackals, and the one about the lion he dismantled with his bare hands. He was particularly fond of bragging about smiting the thousand Philistines hip and thigh because he saw it made me shiver uncontrollably. He liked to kiss and pet me then, I submitted with the sound of wet cloth tearing in my ears.

Soon, the matter of his secret became more urgent. War was in the offing, and not much prospect of victory for us. Whole regiments blanched at Samson's long hot stare full of the red rage ready to leap out. And who could blame them? Not I, who knew him. There was nothing for it but to invoke the protection of the Good Goddess and go to bed with Samson. For the record, sex with him was no picnic. He had some very peculiar fancies. He liked to be tied up with ropes, and then I had to go to the door and shout, "Samson, the Philistines are upon you!" and with one mighty bound he would break free of his ropes and leap on me. He explained that this was just one of his little jokes, but it was no joke. Believe me, I know. Bed had to be as much like the battlefield as he could make it, and I as much the enemy. Pain was the only thing which aroused his lust. There were times when I stood gibbering at that door with my nails bitten up to the elbow with fright, praying he wouldn't be seized by the spirit of the Lord and a fancy for something more terminal. He came close sometimes.

Then one night when I was combing his long hair and gossiping about some new diet for musclemen, he yawned and said he didn't need anything like that, his strength was in his hair. He rolled over and fell asleep. Just like that, the nation's ordeal, and mine, was over. I took up my manicure scissors and gave him a short back and sides. Just for the record, I didn't shout, "Samson, the Philistines are upon you", I whispered that Delilah was, and as I snipped off his hair, tress by tress, I said, "This one for Ashtorek, and this for the children we never had, and this for the dead on the moors, and this for the hungry babies and all the other useless mouths who didn't make it". All his chickens came home to roost at the same time, you might say.

The daughters of the Philistines rejoiced that night. There was dancing in the streets and all kinds of celebrating. It was relief, and the idea that the future was so much brighter and cleaner without Samson's shadow looming across it. I was the darling of the Philistines and the toast of the town.

The first sign of something nasty in the woodpile was when the court painter was commissioned to paint a mural for the victory feast. His disappointment when he saw me was obvious. Not his most inspiring subject ever, his expression told me, but he was a willing soul, and in the end, the picture showed me scarlet-lipped and voluptuous and seething with dangerous sex. Samson was all bronzed and noble, trapped in a net of gold at my feet, the very model of a tragic hero. Every picture tells a story, and I didn't like this one. The Delilah in the picture, had she a shred of decency, should have been looking down at that handsome agonised face and promising abjectly that she would never, ever let it happen again. "Artistic licence," the painter said. "It's what your public expects, dear".

Which was all very well for him to say, but what was my mother going to make of it all?

I was right not to like the picture. Everyone who mattered came to the victory banquet – the city fathers, the captains and the kings, the heroes and the page boys, and the court jester. I was the only woman, and about as welcome as a bed bug. I had encroached on their territory by saving the country, but I stuck it out. I had earned my place at that table.

The wine circled, the men grew flushed, and the first mutterings began. No way for a soldier to go, was it? Man like that should have gone down fighting. None of us are any match for a scheming woman – minds like corkscrews and no idea of fair play. There was a lot of that kind of thing, the gist of which was that what I had done wasn't quite cricket, and wasn't it just like a woman to play dirty pool? Samson might have been a devil, but at least you knew where you stood with him. He had a frank and manly way with him, never did anything underhand, you had to respect that about him. In short, I was not quite a gentleman, and very far from being a lady.

The jester had a field day. Personally, I found him very unfunny, but many of my table companions took on a musing and speculative air as they looked at me. Clearly, there was more to me than met the eye. Had to be, hadn't there? One old general actually offered me a bag of gold to spend the night with him, accompanied by a round of applause from all present. Samson earned more kindly stares than the one I got when I refused. Anyone would think I was the mortal enemy who had to be overcome. Ah, if only I had done something frank and manly like murder or arson, then I could have been a hero too.

But things being as they were, I didn't stay long in the valley after that. The Israelites were forming stoning parties, and my popularity with the Philistine men was downright embarrassing. So I missed the postscript when Samson brought the temple down on all their heads. They should have known better than to bait him like that, but they just had to have their share of Samson's defeat. Men say that Samson's god had the last word after all. They forget that the Good Goddess has a long memory; through me, her protection was despised and she was insulted.

At any rate, I live in another country where everybody knows what Delilah is, but nobody knows me. The Goddess looks after her own, and someday when the dust has settled and everyone has forgotten all about it, I'll get home to my home in the valley.

Illustration by Trish Edwards

Imaginary Friends

Laura Hird

Mr Paterson was like no other adult she'd ever met. She'd only known him for three Wednesdays but already they were best friends. When her last piano teacher had gone on holiday to Blackpool and not come back she hoped she wouldn't have to take lessons any more, but now she had Mr Paterson she practised all the time without her mother even having to tell her.

He had a lovely, big, fluffy dog called Caliban which he said she could take for walks. Her mother wouldn't let her at first but after a few days pestering she agreed, as long as she did it before tea as a girl in the year below her at school had almost been stolen by a car the other week. She'd always wanted a dog of her own but her mother said they were a nuisance and her father sneezed. Mr Paterson said she could come and see Caliban whenever she wanted because no child should be without a pet. He also gave her sweeties and fizzy juice and told her they weren't really bad for your teeth. Parents only said that to punish children.

She thought he was great. He'd play with her and not get bored, just like her best friend, Mark, but because he was an adult he knew what they were like – how they pretended all the things she liked were bad for her, how they said there was a bogey-man just so she couldn't play outside at night, how they only sent her to school so they could play all day when she wasn't there.

She'd turned up crying for her last lesson with him because a big girl at school had hit her for hiding her schoolbag in the toilets. The girl was always bullying her and she thought if she stole her bag she might stop but instead she'd pulled her hair and scratched her and thrown her on the ground. Mr Paterson was all nice about it and told her she shouldn't steal anything unless she knew she wouldn't get caught. He'd given her a cuddle then they'd thrown cushions at each other until she got the hic-ups. She didn't even have to play the piano. He just told her to practice extra hard and not tell her mother. But best of all he promised to show her some magic the next time she came round.

She ran to his house after school the following day. He was in the middle of giving a lesson so she took Caliban for a walk but was back at his door within minutes, desperate to see some magic. He laughed when he saw her there so quickly and ruffled her hair: "You can't wait, can you?"

He led her into the kitchen, sat her at the table with some comics and a milk shake and left her with the dog while he finished giving the lesson. She looked around at his things but didn't touch – not that he'd mind but he was still an adult. There was a photo stuck to the fridge of him with a lady and a little girl, younger than her. They all looked very happy and it made her feel a bit sad but she didn't know why.

When he came back through he saw her gazing at the photo and pointed at it. "That's my wife and little girl. Her name's Miranda."

His fingers rested on his wife's face. She walked over to have a closer look but the picture made her feel odd so she looked up at him instead.

"Where do they go during the day?"

He smiled and squeezed her shoulder. "Oh, they don't live here any more. We're divorced. They stay in England."

Gosh, divorced! She thought only famous people could afford to get divorced. At least that's what her mother said when she'd been shouting at her dad. "They don't stay in Blackpool, do they?"

He held her hand and his eyebrows went wavy. "No, why? What's special about Blackpool?"

She told him about her old piano teacher going there and her mum saying she wasn't coming back. When her and mum and dad went there for their holidays she never wanted to come home but they only ever stayed for two Fridays but when her old piano teacher and her Auntie Agnes and her hamster had gone there she'd never seen them again. Auntie Agnes had been really ill in hospital for ages, then one day she'd gone to visit her with her mum and she'd gone off to Blackpool. Why would a sick, old lady want to go there?

He laughed and made her another milk shake than sat down opposite and stared at her like she was a picture. "There's a lot of magic in Blackpool. Did you know that?"

She felt all excited. He took her hand again and continued. "Yes, in the fairground, on the pier, even in the Tower. It's a magical place. That's why there's all those lights. They use the power from all the magic as electricity."

It all suddenly became clear to her. She'd always known Blackpool was a special place.

"I suppose you'll be wanting to see some magic now?"

She nodded her head enthusiastically and grinned at him. He stood up and took a bottle of clear, purple liquid from the kitchen cabinet and a box of matches from the drawer. "First we have to summon the firebird..."

She giggled, "What the what?"

He handed her the matches, rolled up his sleeves and stood over the sink pouring the purple liquid onto his hands and arms. "The firebird. Once you've seen it you'll be one of the secret society. You won't be able to tell."

He poured more liquid onto himself then asked her to light a match. There was a strong smell like her grandfather's feet. She struck the match three times before it lit. He stood over it and she jumped back as his hands became engulfed in flame. He joined his thumbs and wagged his fingers as if he was making shadow pictures on the wall.

"Do you see it? Do you see it?"

She looked into the fire and gazed at his hands. His fingers were blurred by the flames but as she stared she slowly saw the firebird appear, fluttering in the middle of it all. He was almost shouting now, "Do you see it?"

"Yes, yes, I see it," she giggled, banging her straw into the milkshake.

He blew on his hands and the flames vanished then he pulled a face and said the F-word. He looked at her and smiled, breathless. "I think the firebird bit me!"

He explained that now she'd seen the firebird and was part of the secret society, she couldn't tell anybody about it. If she breathed a word to anyone about the magic they were going to do together, the secret would be broken and he'd lose his magic powers. She swore to tell no one, indeed, she felt important to be a member of the secret society and begged him to produce a rabbit or a white pigeon from somewhere. He told her he could only do one piece of magic a day during the Summer or his powers would weaken. They were stronger in the Winter because Jesus was born then and it was Jesus who first invented magic. Just as Jesus had turned water into wine and raised the dead, Mr Paterson could summon the firebird.

He was sorry to disappoint her though, and asked if some chocolate would make up for it. It was only an hour until tea but as everything was now secret between them she sat on his knee as he scooped the thick chocolate spread from the jar and they licked it off his fingers. He told her if she was good, and didn't tell anyone, then in the Winter time when his powers were strong he'd teach her how to fly. She was overjoyed. She imagined flying off into a tree when the big girl at school bullied her or her mother tried to smack her. She'd show them! He bounced her up and down on his knee and gave her a kiss then left her to play with Caliban and went into the toilet for ages.

She rolled about on the floor with the dog, tickling its huge, fluffy belly, dreaming about all the things they'd do when she could fly then she heard funny noises coming from the bathroom. She calmed the animal down and listened. She could hear Mr Paterson breathing loudly and the occasional little moan, like he was going into trance or something. She began to feel a bit scared in case he'd taken ill or something but just as she was about to knock on the door he came back through to the kitchen, smiling.

He held out his hand and showed her some white stuff that looked like liquid soap. He told her it was special potion and if she drunk it her mother wouldn't be able to tell she'd been eating chocolate or playing with matches. He moved it closer to her face. It didn't look very nice. Like that horrible stuff on top of fried eggs that her mum said was the dead chick. She pushed his hand away, laughing and pulled a face.

"I can rub it into your skin instead. That works just as well. Do you want me to?"

"It looks horrible."

He sat on the settee and asked her to come and stand between his legs.

"It helps you keep secrets and it'll make you feel nice too."

She walked over to him and he tugged her t-shirt out of her trousers with his free hand and lifted it up to just under her arms. She expected the potion to feel cold but it was just normal and as he'd said, it did feel nice as his big hands rubbed it slowly onto her tummy and chest and back. He made her watch as it slowly disappeared into her skin.

"See, it really is magic!"

He gave her little kisses on the back of her neck and shoulders that made her feel all tingly, and told her that this meant that the spell was completed successfully. Then he made her promise again that she wouldn't tell anybody, not only because he'd lose his powers but because if the magic got into wrong people's hands they might use it to do bad things. She promised, thanked him several times for letting her in the secret society, and said she had to go for her tea. He kissed her on the side of the neck, gave her a magic lollipop and told her not to come round for a couple of days in case her mum got annoyed.

She felt sad but smiled until he closed the door, then walked home in tears. Two days seemed like the longest of times. She didn't want to leave him, or Caliban. She didn't want to go home and eat horrible vegetables and pasta then be forced to read some boring schoolbook.

Her mother smacked her when she got home and told her the next time she walked the dog she had to come home and say where she was going first. She could only eat some of her tea as she felt sick from all the chocolate and milk shake, but her mother forced her to finish her broccoli before she left the table. Mr Paterson didn't force her to eat things she didn't want, but then again, he'd never offer her something as revolting as broccoli in the first place. She often wondered if her mother found things lying in the garden and made her eat them just to be nasty.

She had to spend a whole hour on her awful project on Germany and all the horrible people who lived there, then she went next door to see her friend, Mark and play action men with him. She wanted to tell him about the firebird and Jesus inventing magic but she was scared that Mr Paterson would lose his powers and she wouldn't learn to fly in the Winter.

She cried herself to sleep for the next two nights because she missed him so much. She wanted to run away with him and Caliban and be his magician's assistant and have him stick swords through her and then say, "Only kidding". She wanted to rescue him from a car crash then take him home and sit on his knee and kiss him.

She practised the piano especially hard so she could impress him at her next lesson. After a very long two days she went round to his house again. He was talking to one of his pupil's mothers so he gave her the dog and told her to come back in half an hour.

She ran up the street, laughing and smiling with Caliban bounding at her side. She felt all happy and safe now that she'd seen him again. She climbed through the hole in the fence of the wasteground at the top of her street, tied the dog's lead to a piece of rusty pipe that was sticking out the ground and climbed to the top of her favourite tree. She waved down at Caliban and shouted his name. The dog pranced about, barking, pulling at its lead and waggling its tail. She wished she could fly down, pick it up and take it up to sit on the tree with her. She couldn't wait until Winter. It would be just like that film about the snowman she'd seen on the telly.

When she took the dog back the lady had left. Mr Paterson looked a bit worried as he led her through to the living room. She asked him what was wrong. He sat down on the settee and smiled at her.

"It's nothing. That lady was just a bit annoyed, that's all."

How could anyone possibly be angry with him? She didn't know what to say so she knelt on the floor and started playing with the dog. He lit a cigarette and took a deep puff. She'd never seen him smoking before but it looked nice. He looked at her, worried again. "You haven't told anybody, have you?"

"Of course not!"

He smiled again and opened his arms. "Don't I get a cuddle then?"

She crawled across to him and stood up. He put out his cigarette, squeezed her really tight and rubbed his nose on her neck. She stroked his hair, so glad to see him she felt like crying. She liked being cuddled. Her parents had stopped cuddling her last year. They said that seven was too old for cuddles as people might get the wrong idea. They did say the oddest things sometimes. Eventually he released her and she knelt at his feet. He played with her hair and stared at her sadly. "Have you been thinking about me?"

She held his hand and looked back at him, her eyes twinkling.

"Yes, I've been thinking about flying. I wanted to ask you about it."

"Uh huh?"

"Well, if people see you flying, don't they know you're magic? Won't the firebird die because they'll know the secret? Won't you lose your powers?"

He told her it was alright. Before you flew you put on an invisible suit so the only people who could see you were people in the secret society.

Invisible! Think of all the things she could do if she was invisible. It got better and better. She asked him where he would get the invisible suit and he said he kept some on top of his wardrobe. She pleaded with him to let her try one on, just for a few minutes. She wouldn't ask him to do any more magic today, just, please could she try one on. Just to see what it was like?

He stood up and kissed the top of the head. "You're terrible, you know that? I shouldn't really do this until Winter."

He went into the bedroom and came back through with a suitcase which he laid on the floor in front of the settee and sat down again. "You'll have to take your clothes off though."

She looked up, shocked and asked him why.

"Because it only makes people invisible, not their clothes."

She sat on the floor, not quite knowing what to do. She felt a bit strange about getting undressed but she knew she could trust him and he wouldn't tell anybody because he'd seen the firebird too. She began taking her clothes off slowly. He sat watching with his hands in his pockets. She stripped to her pants then hesitated and looked at him again, her face red.

"Do I have to take everything off?"

He raised his eyebrows. "Well people would think it a bit strange if they saw a pair of knickers flying about the sky. It's OK. I have got a wee girl, remember?"

She took off her pants then stood looking at him. He smiled and gestured to her.

"Come and sit here for a minute. I want to talk to you."

He lifted her onto his lap and began kissing her neck and shoulders and chest. "These are magic kisses. They make sure people can see you again when you take the suit off."

He continued kissing her until Caliban began barking at the window. He looked up to see what was wrong then the doorbell rang. He stood up suddenly and she fell onto the carpet. He helped her up.

"Sorry, are you OK? I don't know who it is."

She felt panicky and began picking her clothes off the floor.

"What'll I do? What about the firebird?"

He rushed her into the bathroom and told her to get dressed and not to come out until he told her. She was in there for ages. The doorbell rang another five times, each time longer than the last, then stopped. For a while she couldn't hear any noise. She was scared. And then she was bored. She waited and waited until finally he opened the door and peered in.

"Are you alright? I think they've gone."

She walked out the bathroom. "Who was it? I have to go home for my tea. Mum'll kill me."

He walked through to the living room and sat down on the settee without saying anything. His body was shaking so she took his hand. It felt all cold and damp and made her arm vibrate it was trembling so much. He put his other hand on her shoulder and looked into her eyes. "I think the magic's in danger. I think the people who were at the door have found out about it."

She felt frightened. She imagined the belting she'd get off her mum if she found out. She imagined there being no more magic in the world and it being all her fault. What would happen to Caliban?

"But how did they find out? I didn't tell anybody."

He didn't answer. He was thinking. Finally he looked at her again.

"I think I'll have to put the invisible suit on for a while. Until they stop looking. And Caliban too."

She felt like she was going to cry. "But what about me?"

"Well, if I'm invisible I can be with you all the time. Nobody'll know…" He cuddled her, "as long as you remember the firebird and keep it secret."

He told her she wouldn't even have to speak to him, just think and he'd be able to read her mind. She could finally have a dog and her mum and dad wouldn't even have to know about it. He told her he would keep the suit on until the next time she went to Blackpool then he'd come back and they could do magic on the pier and fly off the top of the Tower together. She felt it was going to be alright. All her dreams were coming true.

He wasn't shaking as much now. He went to the toilet for a little while to look for the potion then came back and rubbed it into her so no one would know their new plan. He told her it would be better if she went out the back door in case the people who'd come for the magic were still outside.

He lifted her onto the wall between his garden and the street, told her she was his best friend and that he and Caliban would be with her when she fell asleep then she dropped onto the pavement and ran all the way home.

By the time she turned into her road she wasn't scared any more as she sensed Mr Paterson and Caliban were already with her. When her mother smacked her she was brave and didn't cry because she knew they were watching. She spent the weekend in her room playing them all her favourite records and having conversations in her head and two days later, when her mother said that one of the neighbours had told her that Mr Paterson had disappeared she laughed in her head and heard him laughing back.

Valerie Thornton

Shadows

In this thin-walled summer night
we touch tips and sip pleasures
with the quiet certainty
of our way towards sleep.

We are shadows
shifting as softly as the curtains
at the open window,
when the wall begins to speak.

We slow to hold,
and hear the rhythmic beat
and sharp words
as his drink curses her drink.

Her moans grow to keening
as he hits harder and faster.
She screams at the final blow
before whimpering to an end.

It is over, for tonight.
We curl together in fragile comfort
aching to stroke and soothe,
knowing our time will come.

Now

Some days I sit
and be old.
I close my eyes
and be very still.
For long.

I think back
to how it was now
and am calm
at all its passing.

When I open my eyes
the world is bleached
like old bones
on pale sand
and I am worn away
with this age-old memory.

Margaret

I think I learned about babies
from Margaret.

She had blue eyes
and cried when I laid her
on her tummy
and howled in hiccups
when I shook her.

Her hair came off,
that is, I pulled it off
in a fit of curiosity
and laughed myself silly
at her baldness.

Her rigid feet resisted shoes
and her arms curved stiffly
into five-pronged tridents
which gave me nightmares
and sore ribs
when I rolled my dreams
on top of her.

I think Margaret still lies
in a cupboard in my head
puncturing dreams of babies
before I impale myself
on motherhood.

Phillip Whidden

Ode to an American Marine from Bountiful, Utah, Killed in the Gulf

> *When in eternall lines to time thou grow'st*
> *So long as men can breath or eyes can see,*
> *So long lives this, and this gives life to thee.*
>
> Sonnet 18

I

So here is what I give you: hero for
A title – which is better than the one
For this parade of words – but poor, quite poor
Of course, considering, then, instead of fun
For your young body (your young buddies guess
My meaning... can still snigger, right or wrong)
A funeral attended by the press
With mists of words, words, words, incense and song;

Our best obsequiousness, this champagne
Of modern courtesies, we give you – see
Your TV coverage? Well, we admit
You don't. Still your father, stoic debris
Beside your coffin, talks with eyes of grit
About the worthwhile nature of your death
While others (mother and brother) refrain
From trying to make it rhyme, save their breath.

II

A few days earlier we even saw
Your teachers on the box. How clean they stood,
In suits and earrings, speaking in an awe
They always had but never knew they should
Have felt when you were in the classroom or
Strolled, laughing, through the noisy open plan.
Today a silence fills the corridor.
This silence has no cadence, does not scan.

The cameras showed your uniform and you
Surrounded by a frame of gilt there on
The mantelpiece and suddenly this view
Brought home the harshest harm from what has gone,
For every lineament of eye and cheek and skin
Cried out as poems never can that boys
Are larger than America. Your chin
Was an impeachment against poets' noise.

III

Hero? It's such a 1950s term,
So square. No sleek Tornado mission has
Ever been that neat.
        Well.
              Your crew-cut sperm
Would not have sought geometry, but as
Unpredictable as the deaths of Scots
In friendly fire would have scorched its way in
Women. How it would have burned, and in lots
Of them, too – given your face, strong as sin
And as taut as the rectangle round that
Photograph. We still see those eyes, that straight
Stare. Technology turned you into... flat
Image. This was before we made your date
For the war and TV crews round the world
Converged on your Mormon town. But for whom?
Not for your mother. On her lap a furled
Triangle, stripes and stars, points to her womb.

IV

So why have I decided I will give
These verses out? It has to be because
Not one of us you left behind can live
Your life for you. That is the thought that gnaws
Away at time. And since we cannot stain
The universe with all that you have lost
And should have done, and since the serried pain
You left in place of life, though beyond all cost,
Is cheap in lieu of you, I have to make
These inexpensive stanzas, lest we
Presume that there is something rich to take
To you there in your grave, some fragrant fee,
Like myrrh and aloes, which might put a stop
To that haemorrhaging *not* shown on our screens,
The desert blossoming in rows of crop-
Like death planted by laser-sure machines.

"And all the sons of God shouted for joy"

The memory of you cleanses even light.
Though clouds today add gray to sky and air
This flashback makes white flowers cleaner white;
I wash them in an essence of dark hair
Poured out in curling moments long ago.
A reminiscence of the laughing way
You walked then purifies the falling snow.
Nothing is cleaner gone than yesterday.

We were light, we two, in the distant past,
But light from distant points is light the same:
Forever shines clearer than the ether.
We were music, a duet, in the vast
Ravines between the spheres. I knew your name
Before the morning stars sang together.

Lot's Wife

I dare to let my face look behind, I
Give my eyes to incinerate with sins.
Must we all abjure the guilt that makes us?

It grips us, coiling like a double helix;
to separate, to untangle is not
an option So, should we shiver,
Longing for incestuous escape, or
Should we turn and listen to elegies
Of ash?

The plains of the past are shining,
Incandescent like memories in black-light brine.

Why am I transmogrified to salt?
I chose the holocaust, preservation.
If murder looks like martyrdom,
If murder, even by a jealous god, crystallizes
It cries out, becomes eternal.

              Why stumble towards
The cave holes of perpetuating slime?

Playing the Shadow Card
Hunter Steele and Black Ace Books
Thom Nairn

I first encountered the work of Hunter Steele a bit late in the day, with the publication of his fourth novel, *Lord Hamlet's Castle* (Andre Deutsch, 1987). Still that book offers as accurate an indicator into the nature of both Steele's work and character as you could hope for. His fiction, along with his inclinations in general, cannot be fitted into any cosy box or "classification"; a good point to move out from.

Lord Hamlet's Castle takes the skeleton of Shakespeare's *Hamlet* and gives the bones a pretty radical shake-down. Along with the "fiction" itself Steele delights in playing with and delving deeply into history and, if both begin to seem precarious, "reality" too tumbles rapidly in their wake. Surreal is closer to the mark, tongue in cheek and punctuated with a raw often bizarre strain of sexual exploration. A few touchstones come to mind you could try Eco, with the rat-run warrens of Elsinore recalling the labyrinthine library of *The Name of the Rose* (similarly, the detective story/thriller angle), from there perhaps to Alasdair Gray's *Poor Things*, a touch of Marquez or Allende and on to Palliser's *Quincunx*. But these are really only suggestive territories. Steele is every bit as distinctive and original as the writers bounced around above. In common with Gray in particular though, Steele displays a love of language, at once extravagant and meticulous; even (almost) offstage these inclinations are given free reign. What I like about Steele's work is that he is so clearly enjoying himself. The quote below for instance is from his brief preface to *Hamlet's Castle*, offering his justification for pursuing his "interpretation":

> --- the bones of the story, the subterranean struts and motivational frets, in all their lustful viciousness, their erectile sensuality, have never been completely bared before.

At this stage all seemed to bode well he had already forged a distinctive style and technique and had four novels under his belt as well as a huge work under way, but things didn't turn out to be quite as simple as that. For some time Steele had been growing increasingly disenchanted with diverse aspects of the established publishing world. This came to a head over the handling of Steele's fifth novel, *The Lords of Montplaisir*, which in hardback (eventually) ran to 696 pages but was crunched in Macmillan's earliest draft into 549 pages, resulting in an ugly, virtually unreadable text which Steele refused to thole.

In the wake of this experience Steele and his girlfriend Boo Wood set out to try to pin down a different way of doing things. Having made up their minds, they didn't muck about and in 1991 founded their own Black Ace Books, undertaking from then on to tackle the whole shebang themselves. Black Ace have subsequently maximised the potential of developments in technology over the last ten years or so: highly efficient hardware and software, still rapidly evolving to expand possibilities, enabling Black Ace to produce impressive publications "from home". They have also developed their own answers to sales and distribution, employing targeted mail-shots/mail-order with hardback publications while marketing their paperbacks in bookshops themselves.

Black Ace have now published a fair number of books aside from two works by Steele himself and their catalogue already displays an intriguing eclecticism, perhaps not too surprisingly reflected in the range of Steele's multifarious undertakings. Aside from his work as a novelist and now publisher he also makes forays into journalistic work.

He also produces song lyrics and short stories, the latter essentially microcosmic flashes of his larger works, while, tucked away but as yet unpublished, there is *The Four Moral Dimensions*, a "development of the ethical theory of the German Idealist Arthur Schopenhauer".

Moving on, though, Black Ace Books *are* impressively produced. Their two initial publications, for instance, Alwyn Clark's *An Enlightened Scot* (a life of Hugh Cleghorn) and Steele's lyrics and stories in *Crumbs of Love* (both 1992), are sewn hardbacks printed on fineblade paper with colour endpapers.

However, a well produced book is always a pleasure to lay hands on but, at the end of the day it's what lies within that really matters. The books I have in front of me are all radically different in terms of form, style and content, each though in its own distinctive ways a pleasure to read. I began with Steele's *Crumbs of Love*, the lyrics and stories as well as a selection of workshop ideas and techniques. Although the book looks good, featuring delicate and appropriate illustrations by Mary Ruth Craig, I was a little sceptical about the entire concept; as Steele himself observes at the outset, "Not all song lyrics read well as verse". The simple, obvious answer is as I quickly found, don't approach them as verse. You don't read Dylan or MacGowan or Brecht for that matter like that (if you're wise) and you don't need to here.

All in all the book is light hearted, if sometimes sad, and it doesn't pretend to be anything else. One aspect of the book I like is its texture, moving through different lyric forms, stories, illustrations and essays. The essays included as "appendices" cover ground such as "Creating Lyrics" and "Cliche Breaking" and offer a source of approaches for anyone interested or involved in the promotion or generation of creative writing in schools or in a workshop or writers group.

Totally different is Mercedes Claraso's first novel *Natana*. Little mysteries and anticipations sustain the narrative in a style that is very much alive, direct and deceptively light of touch. It is a hard book to put down and it says much for Claraso's craft that she holds you from start to finish while at the same time her two central male characters are so calculatedly boring they're infuriating, a strategy which could have rebounded badly on the book, but doesn't. Both Philip and Clive are accomplished academics, in "good" jobs, extremely unhappy, bored, dull and painfully pedantic to boot. However it is the elusive, other worldly appearance of Natana

(Philip's ex-wife's daughter by a Catalan artist) who edges a way into Philip's life. Her presence is catalytic, regenerative, offering a spark of life, of wonder and redemption, centrally, what the book is "about". But if *Natana* is concerned with rejuvenation, rebirth, it is also a painful study of failure Philip begins to wake up:

> Philip came to the conclusion that his life must be very dull. Nothing else would account for his present reaction to the situation. He hadn't actually noticed that it was dull. But that in itself, the not noticing, was probably just part of the dullness.

The book's jacket notes cite Spark as a reference point and this is pretty accurate, particularly so in the use of a peculiarly complex logic expressed in disorientatingly simplistic terms, a tactic employed tellingly by Natana to bamboozle the hopelessly grasping mind of Philip:

> It was simply a matter of what you see or what you don't see. You can't stop seeing something that's there simply because seeing it leads to problems with the partially blind.

Natana (1993) is a crisp funny, sensitive first novel that has a habit of not taking the directions you might anticipate. Claraso's second novel *Kintalloch* is already available from Black Ace as is her collection of short stories, *Teresa's Decison*, while her third novel, *The Hawthorn Hedge*, appeared in December 1995.

David Daiches' *A Weekly Scotsman* gathers 75 poems from over six decades. The work is chronologically ordered and presented in seven sections, from "Early Poems" through to the concluding "Afterthoughts", allowing us to follow the writer's development, influences, preoccupations, the movements of his thoughts. Edwin Morgan has suggested that the qualities which converge to create a poem are 50 percent earned, 50 percent given. Some of these poems are worked just a bit *too* hard. In his introduction Daiches writes: "for me, however, all art was order, form, pattern, and aimless 'splairging' was the antithesis of art". One of the best, most forceful poems here is "Orpheus and Eurydice" and while this is hardly "splairging" the poem benefits from the easing of structural formality, allowing the bare words themselves to impact more sharply:

> What was it like down there? Have you read
> Any good books lately? What shall we do
> Tomorrow? I know a nice place
> For lunch. Knowing she was listening
> He would have kept her real, kept them both real.
> Rebuilding little intimacies.
> Love is like that.

This, with its wry humour, its fluid construction and the hard cut of reality biting home in the twist of the last line shows Daiches at his most incisive, fluent and flowing.

However, a work of a totally different nature is particularly welcome from Black Ace: a revised edition of Ron Butlin's *The Sound Of My Voice*, originally published by Canongate in 1987 and produced by Black Ace in 1994. The new edition features a fine introductory 'essay' from Randall

Stevenson, one of the few critics, along with Gavin Wallace (see *The Scottish Novel Since The Seventies*), to have taken full notice of the novel and draw attention to its worth (and its neglect). Stevenson relates the book to Malcolm Lowry's *Under The Volcano* and I've no argument with that.

The Sound Of My Voice focuses on the 'life' of Morris Magellan, not a good environment to inhabit. Morris is, among other things, an alcoholic; as Stevenson puts it, he is *not* dealing "with the dark legacies of his childhood", neither does he back off from handing them on to his own family.

He's chasing a panacea which only offers darkness at the end of his own particular tunnel. But, for all that darkness there is too a bizarre humour at the core of the novel which enables it to become "something" you may not expect. Here perspectives, notions of reality, flicker alarmingly. Morris thinks he's dealing with everything perfectly but he's usually wrecked out of his head and everyone knows that except him (most of the time anyway). The novel painfully illustrates everything falling to pieces, roughly, Morris and Reality in tandem.The literary techniques employed amplify and capture Morris's self-delusion: you're embarrassed for him, thinking "don't *say* that", "don't *do* that", "God! don't even *think* that".

In the meantime, though, Black Ace just don't stop. There is the new work from Mercedes Claraso to check out, there are the 696 pages of *The Lords Of Montplaisir* (look out for the boar hunt sequence in the early pages of the novel) as well as Hunter's "Monster" tentatively titled *Succeeding At Sex And Scotland Or The Case Of Louis Morel : A Tale Of Two Or More Mysteries Not Excluding The Novelist's Labyrinth*. And, the chapter titles add up to a poem in themselves: how about "Beyond Satellite Sex", "Tall Dark and Plausible" or "Anal Intercourse, AIDS and Sovereignty in Scotland", just for starters? I look forward to it.

There is much more that should be said: the publication of Lorn Macintyre's *The Waterloo Woods In Retreat*, Steve McGiffen's *On My Way Weeping* as well as Colin Mackay's *House Of Lies*. All books to be investigated as soon as possible, if you can keep up?

War of the Roses

Henryk Skwar

In 1453 Queen Margaret bore Henry VI a son, and two years later the civil war broke out: the Red Rose of Lancaster against the White Rose of York. This story skips a few centuries to the present at the Academy of Gaelic Art in the village of Tworki near Warsaw, where one can conduct a chamber orchestra or play chess with Cyrano de Bergerac.

* * *

"Now you're in the inner circle," his teeth clacked. "In a minute you will join the cuckolded prophets in Mountjoy," he said bending toward me.

"Please call the next person," said the nurse, fumbling among her papers and not looking at us.

"He won't call anybody now," I heard the calm voice of the doctor.

I turned and went out. The man who had been in the doctor's office followed me. Several people were in the lobby. We walked past them. The hospital yard with its leafless trees that looked like scarecrows could be seen through the window. It was getting dark.

"Is Joyce with them?" I broke the silence.

"You mean James?"

"I don't remember his first name, but there must be at least one."

"Of course James is with us," his teeth clacked again. "The council decided that *Ulysses* is a perfect example of modern verse and should be published in seven thousand and two short volumes of poetry. It is also used as an anaesthetic by our doc."

"What do you mean?"

"After reading twenty pages the patient falls asleep."

We turned right and reached a door marked "Operating Room," where a man in striped pajamas was standing. He was fat and knock-kneed, with a beak-like nose. For a moment he raised his right foot, and like emperor Bokassa at his coronation, rubbed it against his left calf. As he heard our steps, he turned and cocked his head. Our eyes met.

"How can I remember the number?" his voice broke. "I've never had a head for numbers."

We stopped.

"You mean the room number?" I asked.

"I'll forget it right away," he groaned. "I have a poor memory."

"1571," I checked what was on the door. "The date of the battle of Lepanto."

"Ask Cervantes, if you forget," added my companion." He lost his hand there. You'll find him in our room."

"1571," repeated Bokassa.

We continued down the corridor. It was dark, though some light emanated from the rooms we were passing.

"What's your name?" I asked.

"Copernicus," he introduced himself. "Nicolaus Copernicus."

"Are you a patient?"

"In a sense we all are," he evaded my question.

"I read your hypothesis."

"*De Revolutionibus Oribium Coelestium?*"

"Published by the underground?"

"The underground," he confirmed. "So, you read it."

"I'd forgotten the exact title. If I'm right, you're not a writer?"

"No, I'm serving here as a subject for a doctoral thesis."

"Don't you think that anarchy and chaos are the basis of our world?"

"You will discover that even here everybody obeys certain laws."

"Oh, it's not my intention to instigate anyone against the gods."

"Some day people you knew will come, and you'll see faces you saw only for a moment," his hands sank into the pockets of his dressing-gown. "You'll stretch your arms out and want to touch them, but will encounter only air. Your mind will be like an aquarium full of plants and colorful, mysterious fishes. You will be able to admire all this only through glass. That will be the moment to start your work, but be certain that real achievements earn the respect only of wise people and are ignored by the general public."

"There's not much time between old age and death."

"Our anarchichal friends thought the same," said Copernicus. "When they found themselves here, they started to appreciate life. They became passionately involved with law and order." He opened the door and said, "Welcome to the place where you can dance Giselle In *Swan Lake* or take part in a space program with Neil Armstrong."

A few people in pyjamas stood in the warm, stuffy room. A chess-board was lying on one bed. Everyone was grouped around it. Heads turned to look at us.

"Paolo," I introduced myself.

"Paolo is already one of us," announced Nicolaus gently, taking me by the elbow. "I was there when he was admitted."

"That's good," said somebody who, I later learned, was Jonathan Swift. "He can be responsible for mailing our petition."

"Most of the people in this room are convinced that poor verse has an adverse effect on the birth rate," Nicolaus began. "In their opinion, all the bad poets should be resettled on Achill Island. It won't be easy. You know how hard it is to get rid of a bad poet, almost as difficultas eliminating a good one. The government of Eire would be compensated by donations from the rest of the world. The resettlement program would be sponsored by the United Nations."

"We worked on the text all afternoon," said Swift, giving me a sheet of paper with writing in blue ink all over it.

"May I sit down?"I asked. "I come from Tipperary way on four tired legs that bid me stay."

"Oh, Paolo is a poet," one of them was genuinely happy. "I used to write poems, too. Now I only charge fees."

"For printed material?"

"Hell, no!" he bridled."They pay because I agree not to publish in their magazines. In that way, they maintain a certain literary level."

"I looked at the paper that Swift had given me. Curiosity drew the rest of them into a circle as I read.

Your Highness:

For the sake of Art, we, the undersigned, would like to ask you, Your Majesty, to single out all bad poets and resettle them on Achill Island. If they resist, we propose to add to their number two or three excellent ones, chosen by a national lottery sponsored by our team of laureates. To smooth the process of resettlement free earplugs should be distributed to the local inhabitants.

There were a lot of signatures; among them Flann O'Brien, Alexander the Great, James Joyce, Cyrano de Bergerac, Niel Armstrong, Miguel Cervantes, Oscar Wilde, Sancho Pansa, Jonathan Swift.

"Should I sign, too?"

"It's up to you," said Nicolaus, giving me his pen.

NOTES MADE DURING MY STAY AT THE ACADEMY

Monday

Today we discussed addictions. Cyrano de Bergerac tried to prove that the number of them is constant. If one is taken away, another appears in its place. Wilde disagreed. In his opinion, the total number of addictions increases as new ones are added. Those that disappear are irrelevant. Swift pointed out that this depended on the addiction.

Tuesday

As I was passing the doctor's office at noon, I heard yells. I asked Nicolaus what was going on. He explained that sometimes there are breaks in the delivery of electrical power and then the doctor uses other tools. "What kind of tools?" I asked. He didn't answer. His silence was worse than his admissions that the doctor's instruments are a saw or a hammer or chisel. Why the hell don't they just apply *Ulysses?*

Wednesday

I sneaked out to the post office and mailed a letter. On my way back I thought about Achill Island. Nicolaus told me he's very skeptical about the results of our petition, especially since our MPs are not very reliable people. He's quite seriously considering emigration, if he can get permission from King Ubu.

Thursday

The nurse gave us chess pieces for our chessboard. I immediately started a game with Maxwell, the dog. Whenever we feel that our blood pressure is low, the doctors threaten to set him on us. Maxwell is well-mannered and cultivated, but you never know what kind of idea will find its way into his head.

Illustration by Stephen Lee

Friday

I talked to Armstrong about his trip to the moon. He is planning something even more exciting now - a voyage to the sun. That should really immortalize him. He told me that almost everything is prepared. I doubt whether the rocket will stand the high temperature of the star and told him so. He was a little embarrassed and admitted that he hadn't thought of that.

Saturday

This morning Cervantes announced that he had been bitten by two mosquitoes in the night. Swift was kicked out of the restroom by Alexander the Great. The fat is in the fire.

Sunday

Today was Visitors' Day. The son of Jonathan Swift, extremely proud of himself, reported to his father that he had saved some money. Instead of paying for the bus on his way here, he ran behind it. Jonathan boxed his ears: "Oaf! Blockhead! You would have saved much more running behind a taxi!"

Monday

At breakfast I talked to Cyrano de Bergerac. He assured me that the director of our academy is a little odd. People chosen by him have to drink more that ten litres of water a day. The results, he keeps saying, will be visible in a few months. The struggle against obscurantism heads Cyrano's agenda for the next couple of years.

Tuesday

Armstrong gave a lecture about flying. Everbody wanted to fly, especially Alexander the Great. Jonathan promised to get him a parachute. He also announced that, according to new studies, lying on the right hip helps humans think faster. Maxwell constantly barked at all of us but particularly at Flann.

Wednesday

Oscar tried to convince Cyrano that nothing is more wonderful than stupidity. Ignorance rules. The form of government most suitable to fools has to be selected by them; otherwise, the whole responsibility for the havoc of real life would be ascribed to individuals like us. Wise people live and die in exile.

Thursday

Today I again played chess with Maxwell. Joyce said, "Paolo, this dog's a real genius." " You're nuts, James," I said with a wave of the hand. "He's just lost his thirteenth consecutive game."

Friday

The director of our institution told us that ducks are the most reasonable and prudent of animals because they drink only water. Soon after, Sancho, who belongs to his experimental team, tried to hang himself. Flann rescued him.

Saturday

Alexander the Great lured Swift out of the restroom with a ruse. Jonathan screamed that the time had come to do away with these big names. According to the latest gossip, Jonathan belongs to a terrorist organization. I slept on my right hip all night. In the morning a spate of thoughts wreaked havoc of my mind. Does it work after all?

Sunday

Somebody brought the news that *De Revolutionibus Oribium Coelestium* will be published in a limited edition. Otherwise, the day was full of quarrels. In the beginning Cervantes argued with Swift. Miguel kept saying that everything is related to everything, Jonathan - that nothing is related to anything. Then Alexander the Great talked about the Scythians. Persians invented seedless grapes, he said, but the Scythians invented foamless beer. It can tapped from barrel to glass and poured back again fifty times without a speck of foam.

Monday

Today journalists visited Cyrano and asked him if he would agree to suffer because of people's ignorance. He told them: "No, thank you, no, I thank you, and again, I thank you." After dinner thuds reached our ears from the corridor and then somebody's gasps and yells. We all ran out of the dining-room to see Sancho lying on the ground with somebody sitting on him and banging his head on the marble floor. We were barely able to drag the attacker away. The attendants brought a straight-jacket and escorted him to solitary. I recognized him as emperor Bokassa whom Copernicus and I had once met in the corridor.

Tuesday

We received a letter from the office of King Ubu. Petition denied. Oscar said that nothing can be done about bad poets, but he has the best presentiments. We discussed the problem till the early hours of the morning. I also found out that by means known only to him Jonathan obtained a parachute for Alexander the Great. Because of that they have declared a temporary truce.

Wednesday

After dinner we all went up to the fourth floor. Alexander the Great, accompanied by our flight expert, Neil, put on the parachute, stood on the windowsill, made the sign of the Macedonian cross, and jumped. We heard a terrible crash. We ran down to the yard and found Alexander screaming at the top of his lungs. Both of his legs had to be put in casts. He didn't want to talk to anybody. Jonathan said that his fall will be a good lesson for future generations. Man's life is short and fame is short as well because it depends on others who will also die soon.

Thursday

The doctors had a consultation about the jump of Alexander the Great. They couldn't figure out what inspired him to fly. Armstrong was investigated. Alexander, who is confined to the intensive-care ward, has a new roommate, the director of our academy. His reason for being there? He insisted that people with water on the brain make the best artists and forced some of our friends to drink tens of litres of it a day to see if it would improve their artistic abilities.

Friday

Sancho's strangulation was cleared up. Bokassa wanted to find out when the battle of Lepanto took place. We asked Sancho why he didn't just tell the poor emperor. He answered that he couldn't be responsible for the deeds of his author. It's Miguel who lost his hand there, and he should remember the exact date. Flann pointed out that I should know why Bokassa was assigned to our academy, but I pled ignorance. He found himself here after the accident with the special envoy of the United Nations who visited our country last year. Bokassa was accused of having had him for dinner, though the affair was never entirely cleared up. It rained all night.

Saturday

Alexander the Great was transferred back to our room. He became quite garrulous and told us how, on his way to Persia, he visited Troy, cut the Gordian knot, and met Roxana. We were amused by his account of a trip through one of the conquered territories in the guise of Dionysus. He said: "The daily feasts were so prolonged that I forgot which army I was commanding and who the enemy was. If someone had persuaded me that I was the ruler of the Persians, I would have been disposed to believe it." He assured us that this is the fate of all aging rulers.

Sunday

We had quarrels before and after dinner. Many visitors came and took part in our arguments. Two camps were formed: pessimists and optimists. The pessimists were Flann O' Brien, Jonathan Swift and Sancho Pansa. The rest were optimists. The optimists kept saying that we will all die. The pessimists insisted that our demise would be quick. After dinner we continued the debate and established an executive committee for the coming anniversary of the Battle of Lepanto. We proposed Sancho as chairman, but he refused. Copernicus accused him of lacking affection for his author. Cervantes, who was with us, didn't comment, though somebody heard him muttering that a good donkey is better than a bad servant. In the evening I played chess with Maxwell. He won his first game. What an impact environment has on our lives!

Monday

Alexander the Great died last night. We laughed all day long, not because he died or because he was an optimist, but because we could think of nothing better to do. Then Swift confessed that he was responsible for Alexander's fall. On that tragic day when Alexander wanted to fly, Jonathan installed a fire- extinguisher on his back instead of a parachute. Some of us were upset that an expert like Armstrong hadn't noticed that.

Tuesday

The day was beautiful and sunny. After the funeral of Alexander the Great we played ballbasket in the garden. I was a member of the same team as Wilde and Copernicus. We played well but lost. Nicolaus calmed me down, saying the history notes many events where the real winners were the losers. In ballbasket the players of one team kick the ball and those of the other chase it with the basket in their hands. A player scores when he covers the ball with the basket. The quicker he does it, the higher the score.

Wednesday

I discussed the rules of history and its mechanisms with Jonathan Swift and Flann O'Brien. The latter insisted that history is based on the constant struggle between victims and autocrats. Jonathan said that humanity can be divided into those who give pointers on how to live and those who have to use them. Isn't the ballbasket match, in which the coach and his assistants know how to play the game much better that any of the players, a prime example of this? The good intentions that pave the road to hell, he concluded, provide the real key to understanding the setbacks of humanity. Then Swift mysteriously vanished. We found him locked in the restroom. He didn't want to open the door, so we forced it. He was standing there with a strange smile on his face, repeating just one word, "Houyhnhnm!"

Thursday

I met Neil Armstrong in the library. He informed me that next Sunday is lift-off for the rocket to the sun. He seemed very excited. I reminded him of the heat problem. A spaceship made of even the strongest material might not withstand the temperature of that star. He assured me that there was nothing to worry about because he will fly after sunset.

* * *

What is the relationship between the War of the Roses that took place a few centuries ago and the events at the Academy? Oh, well. Tell me, then, why a certain goat in Turkey spoke several languages, including Hungarian and Spanish. Or explain the difference between a giraffe and an absent-minded clerk. Or tell me why a certain Galapagos turtle ran like mad to the post office after it won two million pesos in the national lottery. You have a lot of questions? Me too. So what? History has already placed us on different sides of the barricades. In 1453 Queen Margaret bore Henry VI a son, but *Revolutions of the Spheres* was published in 1543. How many civil wars have we had since then?

Eveline Pye

Nasturtiums

All swirling skirts and falling hair
you sweep off into the garden
and then you scatter
shades of flame into the salad bowl:
burning candles, flowers

floating on a sea of green.
You ask me to try one.
I peel off a petal and it clings
to my tongue like tissue paper.
Like a bee I lick

the pollen; a soft dusty yellow.
My teeth crush the tiny seeds
and the flavour of the flower
becomes stronger. Greedy now,
I eat the stem,

and it is full of the peppery femininity
of an Indian Summer. I watch
your red hair shining in the sun and
savour the brand new taste
of a hot flower melting in my open mouth.

Afterbirth

I come back from Brownie summer camp
to a strange car at the door, the electric fire
pushed aside, flames in the grate. Gran
is wedged in a chair, a huge bowl in her arms
as if about to bake a monster cake
with soap and water and Johnson's talcum powder.

She washes the blood off my baby sister. Dad
just sits there, watching her, doing nothing
with his sleeves rolled up, eyes melting in the heat.
Someone throws a parcel of newspapers
into the fire. The living room's an oven.

A generation further on, my sister is wired up
to a foetal monitor shouting "Never Again"
at her half Japanese husband - and as the radio
celebrates fifty years since the first V.J. day
Jeanette Ito pokes her beautiful Eurasian face

Illustration by Jules George

out into the modern, post-war world. This time
some nameless nurse dumps the afterbirth
in the incinerator and destroys it
the way the mind wipes out the worst of pain,
when the ordeal is over.

Leaving Africa

All day, I sit by the waterhole
preparing myself. A hippo senses
coolness in the air, drags her body
out of mud. A leopard comes alive

and falls out of the Baobab tree.
The last Kudu twists his corkscrew horns
up to the sky and heads off into the bush.
It's time to leave the village.

You appear, head shaved in grief
ask me to stay... one more time.
You are shouting and crying as I tie
the child to my back. The landrover

comes in clouds of dust.
A snake discards its skin
and emerges smooth as an eel.
I am quietly peeling off years of love

shedding my black skin. You never see
but underneath, I am red raw
bleeding from the loss of you
slithering in dry sand.

The Lunar Rainbow

I walk down the darkening path
to the Victoria Falls in a wilderness
of bushes, long grasses and vervet monkeys.

Day turns into night, like a flock
of flamingos startled on a land-locked lake.
The sound of beating wings as water falls on stone.

I am on the edge of the chasm
touching the sucking beauty of death
when I see colours in the black and silver sky.

An arc of pale pastel hangs
in the moonlight. I stand all night
staring at the lunar rainbow. I don't want morning.

Reviews

Following a Lark, George Mackay Brown, John Murray, £8.99; *Winter Tales*, George Mackay Brown, John Murray, £15.99; *Orkney: Pictures and Poems*, Gunnie Moberg and George Mackay Brown, Colin Baxter, £20.00

These three books were the last George Mackay Brown saw to the end and even if one were to forget his earlier works such as *Andrina*, *Beside the Ocean of Time* and *The Wreck of the Archangel*, with these three book alone he left us an impressive legacy: two collections of poetry, one a beautiful collaboration with photographer and friend Gunnie Moberg, and broad collection of short stories.

Mackay Brown was always in touch with his surroundings and these books are testament to this fact. As well as showing Mackay Brown's attachment to Orkney, the *Winter Tales* are deeply personal and reflective. 'The Laird's Son' shows a young man enjoying the delights 18th Century Edinburgh society then sent to family estate by an ailing father against his will. After the journey to the islands he discovers a world of unimagined pleasures. This story particularly shows Mackay Brown's remarkable skill as a writer with use of contemporary which is no less accessible than the saga style fo which he is so justly renowned.

Perhaps the finest tale of these enchanting stories is the first, 'The Parafin Lamp'. Here is that sentimental part of Mackay Brown that sees 'progress' as taking us further away from our environment, our past and, ultimately, ourselves. Nevertheless, he acknowledges that one cannot live in the past and gently pokes fun at his character who refuses to see the benefits of electricity and running water.

We also see in this collection some of the familiar inhabitants of Mackay Brown's Orkney. We are given a lively account of Ikey the Tinker's year in Orkney. Being a traveller must be the surest way of knowing your environment. But not all is reflective and the collection ends with the rumbustious fight between Orkneys farmers and the fishermen.

Following a Lark too shows Brown's sense of the islands' past, their Norse heritage. There is also a concern with language and the craft of poetry, these combined in a poem to 'Black Thorbjorn'. He also looks to the future and its poets, and gives them sound advice:

Keep vigil. The tongues flow yet
To rythms of sea and hill.
Deeper that stone, guard,
The pure source, silence.

Also here we find tributes to other poets including Robert Burns. The Hebredean says of Burns: "poetry between boards like caged birds" "poetry should be given on the wind, like a lark or a falcon". How right he is. I am reminded of Mrs Dalloway's cry "What a lark!" Mackay Brown's poetry here is alive, on the wind, and a lot of fun.

In all his writing, whether novels, short stories or poetry, Mackay Brown creates a world based on Orkney and brings to it his profound sense of the islands and their history. The already mythical Orkney is given magical qualities in his stories and poetry. Now for those mainlanders not fortunate enough to have visited Orkney, Mackay Brown with Gunnie Moberg, have created a guide to the Orkney in which he lived and created in his writing without compromising either one.

In the sumptuous *Orkney: Pictures and Poems* they move around the islands like two excited children considering feats of engineering as miraculous as the Knap of Howar: Papay, "the oldest house in Europe" to the more recent Churchill Barriers which removed a foundation of island consciousness. "I am an islander no more!" cries the islander and goes on, if this can be done, then:

Will the stars shine over the islands again?
Will sails fly from shore to shore to shore?

They go on to celebrate Orkney's wild and impressive nature and human inhabitantsts, each one as much a part of Brown's enchanted Orkney as the physical world on which it is based. With fine poems and amazing photographs, we have all been privileged to see the inspiration of one of our finest poets.

Sam Wood

Theatre Roundup

THEATRE'S been going through a rough old time these last few months. It's had to cope with yet another year of stand-still Scottish Arts Council funding - in some instances, the third or fourth successive round of real-terms cuts – it's had to figure out the effects of local authority reorganisation - not only a matter of losing subsidy, but also working out who you're getting that subsidy from. There have also been the twin uncertainties created by the resignations of Ian Brown, artistic director of Edinburgh's Traverse Theatre, and Michael Boyd, head honcho at Glasgow's Tron.

Brown goes to pursue a freelance career once he completes his eight-year reign at the end of the Edinburgh Festival. Boyd has already left to take up position as associate director at the RSC. The Traverse ended six-months of speculation with the announcement that the in-house candidate, 32-year-old Philip Howard, will take over in the autumn. As I write, no successor to Boyd has been decided, though the rumoured list of those interested is rather more colourful than those reported to have been interested in the Traverse.

Brown and Boyd are good. In the spring, they both reminded us what they were capable of with the revivals of Sue Glover's *Bondagers* by the Traverse and Janice Galloway's *The Trick is to Keep Breathing* by the Tron, two stunning productions that were both invited to the du Maurier World Stage festival in Toronto and took the opportunity for a few extra dates at home. Are we to lose work of this standard, now we have lost these two directors?

We've yet to see Brown's swan song production - Chris Hannan's *Shining Souls* on the Fringe - but Boyd left us with a typically intelligent production - Samuel Beckett's *Endgame* - to remember him by. Thoughtful, funny and despairing, it took a couple of liberties with the sacred Beckett text - a snatch of Elvis midway through, a foray into the audience by Forbes Masson's Clov, the opening lines delivered on cue cards - but the transgressions were in the author's spirit, emphasising his sense of theatre, his love of a joke and his eye for an arresting image. On Tom Piper's beautiful turret of a set, pale blue walls reaching up from a mound of backstage debris, there were fine cameos from a serene Jan Wilson (Nell) and a toothless Phil McCall (Nagg), with Masson and John Castle (Hamm) creating a compelling love-hate double-act, meting out arbitrary acts of cruelty between bouts of backchat and banter. In short, a rewarding endgame to Boyd's own ten-year residency.

Back at the Traverse, the popularity of David Greig's *The Architect* might have had as much to do with supply as with demand (it played in the smallest theatre for a very short run), but was enough of a success to put it back in the line-up for the Fringe. It was a cleverly sustained comedy, and one of the warmest works by an intelligent young writer, but one that kept too many plates spinning to let us all the way into the tragic core of its story of a contemporary architect whose well-meaning designs in the 1960s come back to haunt him.

I was rather more taken by Greig's next project, with his own Suspect Culture company, called *Airport*, a devised study of departure lounges, baggage control and stranded passengers, featuring three Spanish and three British performers, and almost equal helpings of both languages. Scattered with as many aphorisms as an Oscar Wilde play it was both quirkily funny and subtly observant, exposing much about our sense of identity and need for communication. That it was put together in just four weeks is a matter of wonderment.

With so little new work about, the weaker shows tend to come in for an excess of critical abuse, so perhaps I should be brief in my mention of Morag Fullerton's *No Expense Spared*, a Wildcat comedy about local government corruption that omitted to say anything funny, and of Robert Forrest's *Montrose*, an epic drama about the first Marquis of Montrose and the seventeenth century battle to preserve the distinction between covenant and king. Performed by Edinburgh's Royal Lyceum, *Montrose* was dreary and lacking in emotional range. Fortunately, Forrest had the chance to redeem himself soon afterwards when Fifth Estate staged his *Nova* to tie in with the Edinburgh International Science Festival. The play suffered patches of cumbersome dialogue, but for the most part succeeded in the difficult task of finding a human frame for an intellectual discourse about religious faith, Darwinism, the mystery of life and star-gazing.

By far the most exciting theatrical event of the year took place at Dundee Rep where Alan Spence's docudrama about the city's devastating Timex dispute in 1993 was performed by a mixed cast of professionals and community actors. I can't remember seeing a show that seemed so relevant. Pieced together from taped conversations with those involved, *On the Line* was a chronological, blow-by-blow account of the meetings, picket lines and protests of the year-long dispute. In touching on that gut feeling of injustice being done, it stirred up such powerful emotions and hit on so many bitter political truths, showing how the dispute ripped at the very heart of the community, that it was impossible not to be engaged by it. The repeated heckling from the first-night audience was proof enough.

Other companies operating on good form this year (a year in which the smaller, profit-share companies have been in noticeably short supply) include 7:84 Theatre Company, which performed a tremendously acted Scottish premiere of *Angels in America*; Pitlochry Festival Theatre's triumph, Robert McLellan's *The Flouers o' Edinburgh*, has a marvellous cast including Jimmy Logan, Edith Macarthur, Irene Macdougall and Laurance Rudic; and Glasgow's Tramway which commissioned a strong spring series of local and international innovative work, and started to reclaim the reputation it built up under Neil Wallace.

So a year that began with talk of cancellations and cutbacks has struggled to midway stage with a handful of highlights under its belt. A period of reflection more than proliferation, perhaps, but there are signs of activity just below the surface, suggesting that if this crisis turns out to be merely a transitional phase then there will be theatre-makers ready and willing to capitalise on better times to come.

Mark Fisher

FebFest '96

Febfest 96 really managed to capture the atmosphere of its distant relation, the Fringe. The gossip, the faces new and old, the craving of reviews and mad set changes in under ten minutes could all be found at the archetypal Fringe venue the Bedlam Theatre and to a lesser extent at the Netherbow Arts Centre.

With an admirable selection of plays, monologues and physical theatre one of the festival's successes was moving away from its student roots to include plays from international writers. Most shows were of a high standard, largely performed and directed by the Edinburgh University Theatre Co.

Whether intended or not many plays dealt with love and language. The most memorable belonged to the latter group, a devised piece of physical theatre, *Eve*. While assuming that language was hers and not Adam's this is no heavy handed feminist diatribe, rather an explorative, if prolonged, look at the beginnings of language and its effects. Through a combination of movement, professionally performed by Anna Copp and her "shadow", Lesley Kharma - words and music Eve creates language and, like all poets, in doing so gives meaning to her world. When she encounters another language she discovers a frightening and impenetrable world with a meaning she cannot perceive. Ultimately for Eve language is superseded by dance and the language of the body.

Eve develops language unconsciously, whilst the superbly unified cast of David McCreight's *Zero Equals One* are well aware of their linguistic evolution. McCreight seems to be making a difficult departure from *Sex and Death* which dominated last year's Febfest and Fringe at the Bedlam. Claiming to be "the first play to explain the universe, everything in it and all the maths," *Zero Equals One* has aspirations to Stoppard's *Arcadia*. The characters soon discover that "the only theories we've got are based on nothing" and decide to keep their heads well and truly in the sand. Their whingeing is brutally ceased when they are told that language is "a side-effect of having a larynx in your neck and a dictionary in your head." All this, in spite of its humour, amounts to a rather circuitous route to prove the rather pointless theory that in a universe which doesn't make sense, zero does indeed equal one.

Before seeing Alex R. Evans play about the protocol of sex and love in Edinburgh cafe society, *Making Love* you must ask why – surely nothing to do with the claim that "this play contains strong language and nudity"– it is no more than a sitcom of manners with an 18 certificate. Don't get me wrong; it is nothing if not funny and well structured although the performance lost the knee-jerk irony of the script.

The protocol of the date is examined in Archie Lowe's *Me, Her and the Gooseberry*. With the most garrulous start of all the plays in the festival, this was the only play written in a Scots vernacular. The play moves easily from dialogue to monologue as we learn about the grievances of all three characters. It is through these monologues that the cynically written stereotypes are shattered to great effect. Lowe gives us a witty tragi-comedy of the best order.

Fiona Crisp's monologue. *Still Waiting*, showed the isolation and despair of the individual. A depressed young woman, convincingly played by Caroline Moses, tells, as she waits for her psychiatrist, of the paranoia, internal anger and frustration of depression. Despite going beyond credibility at times this is no victim story of Prozac and whingeing and by preferring to deal with the denial of problems by parents and psychiatrists, the script gets well under the skin of its subject.

On a highly original and different tack, Christopher Young's *Ballad of John Wilkes Booth* looks at the pathology of the actor who assassinated President Lincoln. Written as a series of flashbacks as the chief investigator files his report with dialogues between Lincoln and Booth, this is a well structured play with a political angle as Booth is portrayed as a fighter for Southern liberty killing the maker of the American Empire's first conquest.

Sam Wood

Pamphleteer

The Swiss architect Le Corbusier said - "There is no art without emotion and no emotion without passion." To see the relevance of his statement one should look at eight publications from Cloudforms: *Lazarus Rises* by Roger Thorp with drawings by Michael Thorp *No 1*, £3.50, *The Air Between* by Clere Parsons *No 2*, £4.50, *In The Wings* by T.W. Sutherland, *No 3*, £6.95, *Poems of George Oppen*, selected by Charles Tomlinson, *No 4*, £6.95, *The Journal of an Apprentice Cabbalist* by Edouard Roditi, *No 5*, £6.95, *Volcano Smoke at Diamond Head* by Jeremy Reid, *No 6*, £6.95 *A cortège of daughters* by Elizabeth Smithers, *No 7*, £6.95, *Words for contemplation* by James Kirkup, *No 8*, £6.95. All are limited editions and address according to the publisher - "our prevailing spiritual crisis". The title poem of E. Smithers' volume is funereal and fascinating. The last stanza of six lines has the word "dark" thrice. I sure most tutor would say No! No! to that, yet I am convinced that the New Zealand poet was right to do so (on the subject of colours, who has not seen three of the eight Celtic sub-winds: the dark, the black, and the dull-black?). Roditi's

frank account was conceived in 1931, a time of profound crisis in his evolution as a young poet. Jeremy Reid's poems I could read all night on account of the ease in which he gives pictorial splendours - from "The Castle":

a red rose bordered where the grapes
waxed heavily in black ringlets, a mood
somewhere that fitted with our own
speculations, building with grey paper
not stones, and writing poetry

From the same publisher Cloud, 48 Biddlestone Road, Heaton, Newcastle-upon-Tyne, NE6 5SL, comes another series under the title Markings: *Parts of Speech* by Michael Thorp, *No 1*, £3.00, *Falling Flowers* by Emerald Cleve, *No 2*, £3.50, *LINE* by Peter Dent, *No 3*, £3.00, *Confused by Prayer* by Richard Wonnacott, *No 4*, £3.50 and *HOSTAGES* by Jude Weeks, *No 5*, £3.50. The two most accessible are the short story by Jude Weeks and Emerald Cleve's poem-book, where the love of nature is delicately shown. In one aspect flowers range in size from tiny blooms of duckweed to the gigantic Victoria water lily of the Amazon. There is the 17-syllable haiku of Basho, the 50-page long poem "Reynard the Fox" by John Masefield. Flowers are of all kind and poetry is of all kind too. Is there a place today for poems not written exclusively for the world of the academe, but poems written about the rural landscape and real characters of the Border country? Yes, there is, because over the last three years Don Ledingham has found an appreciative audience - in his vicinity and elsewhere, for such poetry. *Langshaw Echoes* is available from D.L. Ledingham, Smithy Press, Smithy House, Langshaw, by Galashiels, £3.50. There are not many Central Belters who could write a poem based on the reality of sheepdog trials, and I have a feeling a poem on sheepdogs by Benji Rogers of London, itself would be something of wundor -

"I leave by the back door or the window" is by Benji Rogers and is hand made by Cassie Rogers. This book is a little beauty, about a love affair possibly, full of intrigue and novel phrases like "a crumpled rill of water", "orange-fruit street lamps", "to colour clean and strange my thoughts" and "lazy un-living candles". To Benji and Cassie down there in the metropolis: I want you to know that we Scots thank you for reminding us that Mystery

is the Superglue of the Universe. Some poems are previously published, which may include the lines from 'Who dreams of sleeping?'

.. I watch you as ghosts
misplaced in pictures misplaced;
and you haven't found me yet?
... I watch you sleep
under a river-less ceiling.
I watch you sleep/ in a sky without stones.

3 x 4, 12, The Equation Complete, has three poems from the four poets Zanna Beswick, Harry Guest, Ian Robinson, and Jay Ramsay. There are poems of substance here for a change – Beswick mentions that Godsend, the Australian architectural feature the verandah – a word from the Sanskrit leid! and Ramsay speaks of stone, the icon and the cloud of morning: "as you blink and look again/– And the years gone, grey stone, like purple lightning/ In the slow steady soundless rising of the dawn." The small sum of £1.50 to 3 x 4, Rauchland Publications, Kingseat, Fife, KY12 0TP would be welcome; I see no source of funding acknowledged and they are keen to publish poets, which cannot be wrong.

Now for the publication everybody should read. Two chapters from a book first published in 1891. *Chapters of Scotch Humour from "Thistle Down"* by Robert Ford, Akros Publications, 18 Warrender Park Terrace, Edinburgh, EH9 1EF, £3.00 For those who think the Scots tongue has no graphic force or power of pathos and humour, read this and gim nae mair. I shall re-tell in English one wee story: an old girl goes into the corner shop and asks for candles. The price of candles to her surprise has gone up due to short supply, because the British are at war with the French. She asks the shopkeeper if it is true that the two armies are fighting in candlelight? The insights into 19th century social conditions, and the humour lead me to say Well Done to Akros.

Harvesting the Edge by G.F. Dutton, Menard Press, 8 The Oaks, Woodside Avenue, London, N12 8AR, £8.99 is a book of high quality on high-altitude gardening that is not without strong clean poetry. The site is the south-east Highlands and G.F. Dutton adds his knowledge of science, mountaineering, literature, and horticulture to write a remarkable, unique book. On heavy snowfall:

I recall one morning when a great many

trees had been shattered, and others were exploding in stillness (for trees burst under stress). The air was acrid with birch juice.

New Verses for an Auld Sang by James S. Adam, The Herald Press, Arbroath, £4.65. Look out for 'Letter from Arbroath' a poem Adam has written in Scots, the letter being the one sent to the Pope in 1320, notable for its use of direct language. Mr Adam has family verses also, sincere tributes to kith and kin.

Two Second Selection and *Worm's Eye View* are by Robert Roberts, a retired dominie, £2.00 each from Pikestaff Press, Ellon House, Harpford, Sidmouth, Devon, EX10 0NH. Please Sir! your pamphlets are under-priced. In a short time Robert has become widely published, proving that well-crafted rhyming poetry is not out of fashion. *Worm's Eye View* has light verse like the opening of "To His Not So Coy Mistress":

For Christ's sake, darling, steady on:
It scares me stiff your sort of fun.
We've hardly even kissed before
You've got us on the floor ...

Second Selection has poems on English poets, one mentioning the 1949 Edinburgh Festival, but on an event in 1987 Roberts says in 'Sunflowers': "Hearing the Chester Beatty 'Sunflowers' by/ Van Gogh had fetched at Christie's just about/ Twenty-five million pounds, amazingly./ I laughed at how those with and those without/ Inhabit different planets."

Grace is an A4 publication compiled by R.L. Cook, judge of the 1994 Michael Bruce Poetry Competition. The winning poem was "Grace" by Kerrie Hardie of Co. Kilkenny: "Sky, then ash trees, then/ hawthorn, rowan, elder. / Cow parsley, wild carrot, chervil, All in full flower./ The scent dredges down ..." Contemporary poets from Ireland, England, and Wales are represented. Kenneth C. Steven - his poem on lambing is excellent, William J. Rae, Michael Venditozzi, Rosamund Beveridge, Helen Bergin, Joanna Murray, Ailsa Cowie, Lindsey Campbell, represent the Scots. The Michael Bruce Memorial Trust, Kinnesswood, Kinross-shire, KY13 7HN have copies of, *Grace*, £3.50. And so my bout of name-dropping comes to a conclusion, as does this review, with the announcement I am going away to read an essay by Douglas Dunn on Hugh MacDiarmid. *Brent Hodgson*.

Catalogue

In April 1929, the American poet Laura Riding drank Lysol disinfectant (such as had recently done for the English poet Charlotte Mew), then jumped out of the fourth floor window of a London house onto a stone area. Her distraught lover, Robert Graves, rushing downstairs, decided to hurl himself out of a third floor window after her. He was almost unhurt, and she survived her severe injuries. Their perverse and intense relationship continued for more than a decade. Riding seems to have been good for Graves's creativity, but was otherwise an utterly self-centred, vain, pretentious and wickedly manipulative pain in the neck. Graves was an interesting man, beside being a wonderful writer, and he deserved the posthumous luck of a sympathetic and acute biographer, his nephew Richard Perceval Graves. *The Assault Heroic 1895-1926* and *The Years with Laura Riding 1926-1940* are now available in paperback (Weidenfeld and Nicolson, £14.99 each) and the same publisher gives us in hardback the third volume, *Robert Graves and the White Goddess 1940-1985* (£25).

Anna Akhmatova was an even greater force in 20th century poetry than Graves. Devoutly patriotic, she lived in Russia during the Stalin years, writing unpublishable poems in honour of murdered and persecuted fellow citizens. Initially a great love poet, she became, as witness to the Terror, in a broad sense, 'political'. Her long-secret sequence 'Requiem' opens:

No, not under the vault of alien skies,
And not under the shadow of alien wings -
I was with my people then, There
where my people unfortunately, were.

Judith Henschemeyer learnt Russian specifically so as to read Akhmatova in the original, and then spent 17 years translating and retranslating her *Complete Poems*, now co-published in an expanded edition by Canongate, with Zephyr Press of New York (£?) The book is enriched by many photographs and portraits of Akhmatova, a notably beautiful woman in youth who rounded into a comely *babushka*.

Most lovers of poetry know about Akhmatova, but how many have read even one Albanian poet? With a population of only three million, Albania, most mysterious and economically 'backward' of European countries, had no standard language till 1972, when an agreed version was drawn, 80% from the Tosk dialect of the south, 20% from the Geg tongue of the north. The standard is now accepted also in Kosovo, part of former Yugoslavia, where an Albanian population lives under gross Serbian oppression, but the capital Prishtine is a major centre of publishing activity, and Macedonia, where Skopje is a focal point for a large Albanian minority. Intriguingly, a medieval form of Albanian, Arberesh, is preserved by centuries-old immigrant communities in southern Italy and Sicily. The national literature of Albania proper was coeval with the late-19th century movement for independence from the Ottoman Empire, but development was impeded by, until the 1950s, four fifths of the population being illiterate. A Unesco-sponsored *Anthology of Modern Albanian Poetry: An Elusive Eagle Soars* (Forest Books, £12.95), translated by Robert Elsie, presents work by 23 modern writers. I cannot say that these English versions sing powerfully to me, but the book introduces a subject that we clearly ought to know more about.

How wealthy, by contrast, Scottish literary culture seems, though our population is outnumbered by the six million Albanian-speakers. It supports, for instance, pleasant little booklets like Louis Stott's *Ring of Word* series, published by Creag Darach, and detailing the literary associations of places in *Stirling and Clackmannan* (£2.95), *Argyll* (£2.95) and *Loch Lomond* (£3.95). I don't think that my life is much enhanced by knowing that Poachy Glen is a Tiny den above Place of Bonhill, which Smollett relates impressed a seafaring neighbour of his in Chelsea as superior to the Pacific island of Juan Fernandez', but Stott does display some erudition. Will he go on to apply it to the South-West? From Daphne Brooke's fascinating *Wild Men and Holy Places: St Ninian, Whithorn and the Medieval Realm of Galloway* (Canongate, £17.99), we learn that by the 12th century "Galloway's bad name ...passed into literary convention." Like Taffy the Welshman, a Gallovidian was by definition a thief. Norman-French Romances represented Galloway as "a very evil land with a very perverse people." These people had a distinctive, quasi-national identity under Lords of Galloway who functioned like independent monarchs. Not till 1235 did the King of Scots tame them. Has any scholar successfully related the region's wicked old character to its emergence in the seventeenth century as the epicentre of diehard Covenanting rebellion?

The Stirling/South Carolina Edition of the *Collected Works of James Hogg*, (Edinburgh University Press) looks most imposing. To *The Shepherd's Calendar* (£29.50), *A Queer Book* (£29.50) and *The Three Perils of Women* (£32.50) is now added *Tales of the Wars of Montrose* (£29.50). These volumes are handsomely designed and expertly edited. They will look good on the shelf - but where? At the prices quoted, few members of the public will purchase them, and one couples warm welcome with the wistful wish that the economics of publishing didn't confine such rediscoveries primarily to university libraries. Canongate's reprint of Fionn MacColla's *And the Cock Crew*, with introduction by John Herdman, costs only £4.99 and one can imagine the curious bookshop browser parting with that on spec and slipping the book straight into handbag or pocket.

Likewise, Canongate Audio's series of recordings of notable works of Scottish literature, at £7.99 per two-cassette box, will attract customers contemplating long car journeys or looking for literary pleasure while they cook. Robert Trotter from *The High Road* reads *The Body Snatcher and Other Stories* ('Tod Lapraik' and 'Thrawn Janet') by R.L.S, and selections of Neil Munro's *Para Handy Stories*. His distinguished *High Road* colleague, Eileen MacCallum, gives us Grassic Gibbon's Mearns stories - 'Smeddum', 'Clay', 'Greenden' and 'Sim', her voice striding beautifully with the poetic metre of Gibbon's prose. I mean 'poetic metre' literally:

An when he cam drunken hame frae the pub
She'd shoo the children out o the room,
Tak off his claes an put him tae bed.

The latest yum-yum in this series is Alasdair Gray himself reading from *Lanark: Volume 1*. The author's fastidious elocution - schoolteacher? meenister? - points his precise prose deliciously. Technically, he reads as well as any actor. I can't say the same for Les Murray, the major Australian poet, whose low-key, throwaway style works far better on a platform, where it's reinforced by the man's vast physical presence, than it does on the cassette produced by The Poetry Business of Huddersfield (£?) But hear his 'An Absolutely Ordinary Rainbow' - proof that living persons can still write great Christian poetry.

Finally, what can one say but 'bravo' as the Mercat Press printing for the School of Scottish Studies of the tunes and words collected by Gavin Greig and the Reverend James Duncan, mostly in Aberdeenshire, early in this century, reaches its 5th and 6th volumes (*The Greig-Duncan Collection*, £35 each, and a bargain) ? 1268 songs so far, many of them with multiple variants. The latest offerings are 'Songs of Love and Marriage' : Volume 6 is described by its editor, Elaine Petrie, as ' the Heartbreak Hotel of the collection. All the broken-hearted come here to brood on their lost chances and shattered lives.' A version of 'There is a Tavern in the Town' (1171), taken by Duncan from Mrs Walker, is such as might have been heard anywhere in Britain any year of the century. But soon after we get five different versions of the words of 'Barbara Allen' (1193). Four seem instantly familiar - yes, of course, that's how it goes. It is wonderful how the structure of a strong song can support so many convincing variants, with that great line, 'Young man, I think you're dying' pointing three of them, while a fourth has 'She said Young man you are dying.' Two stanzas of a fifth version, as sung by Mrs Mutch, were sent to Greig by her neighbour Bell Robertson, and these are unmistakeably North-Eastern:

She met her father in the ha',
Says, Lassie, can ye tak' 'im?
It's time to say Tak' 'im noo,
Fan his grave claes is a-makin.

Greig noted that he'd heard 'The Shepherd Lad o Rhynie'(1194), in Aberdeenshire, sung to the same tune as 'Barbara Allen', which of course was found all over the British Isles. Under 'Auld Lang Syne' (1143), three widely different sets of words show that Burns had no copyright on the famous refrain. And so on . . . . This series is a treasurehouse of interest and insight and sinsight and singsight for scholars and performers alike, and the team of experts, under the general editorship of Emily B.Lyle, who turn it out so impressively, deserve thanks and honours from a grateful nation.

Angus Calder

Prepayment is required. Annual subscriptions: $25, individuals; $45, institutions. Foreign postage: $4.50, Canada & Mexico; $9, outside North America. Single issue price: $7, individuals; $12, institutions. Payment must be drawn on a U.S. bank in U.S. dollars or made by international money order. MD residents add 5% sales tax. For orders shipped to Canada add 7% GST (#124004946).

Send orders to: **The Johns Hopkins University Press,** P.O. Box 19966, Baltimore, MD 21211.

To place an order using Visa or MasterCard, call toll-free 1-800-548-1784, FAX us at (410) 516-6968, or send Visa/ MasterCard orders to this E-mail address: jlorder@jhunix.hcf.jhu.edu

MFS: *Modern Fiction Studies* continues its long and distinguished record of publishing quality articles on prominent works of modern and contemporary literature. Devoted to criticism and scholarship of fiction of the twentieth century, the journal emphasizes theoretical, historical, interdisciplinary, and cultural approaches to narrative. *Published quarterly in March, June, September, and December for the Department of English, Purdue University.*

**WINTER 1994
(Volume 40, Number 4)
Includes:**

- The Novel as War:
  Lies and Truth in Hemingway's
  A Farewell to Arms

- The Eye and the Gaze in
  Heart of Darkness:
  A Symptomological Reading

- Thea Kronborg's Vocal
  Transvestism: Willa Cather
  and the "Voz Contralto"

- Meditation and the Escalator
  Principle (On Nicholson
  Baker's *The Mezzanine*)

- The Figure in the Static:
  White Noise

Notes on Contributors

Marion Arnott: Paisley writer. Work appeared in *Chapman, West Coast Magazine, Scottish Child & Paisley Yarns.* Married with three children.

Angus Calder: Writer, lives in Edinburgh, tired of being best known as author of *The Peoples' War* – aspiring minor poet!

Mark Fisher: theatre critic on *The Herald* and editor of *Theatre Scotland.*

Gerry Cambridge: edits *The Dark Horse,* an international poetry magazine. *The Shell House* is his first poetry collection.

Stewart Conn: lives in Edinburgh. Most recent works are *In the Blood,* and *At the Aviary.* Poet and playwrite, he reviews mainly for *Scotland on Sunday.*

Esther Garke: Born Switzerland, 1944. Studied at Basle and Aberdeen. Has contributed to various Swiss papers and periodicals, and translated a collection of George Mackay Brown's Christmas stories.

Sam Gilliland: born Ayrshire 1939, co-organises Scottish International Poetry Competition. Widely published. Just completed translating Portuguese poet Mário de Sa-Cámeiro's work into Scots.

Paul Harrington: researching Ph.D on Philip Larkin at Glasgow. 'Waking in Spring' is in first collection *Bridges to the Body* which he is currently trying to publish.

Laura J Hird: lives and works in Edinburgh, has been published in *Cencrastus, Rebel Inc.* and forthcoming anthology *The Psychoactive Sync.*

Brent Hodgson: Born New Zealand c. 1845! Submits poetry & fiction to literary outlets regularly as the sight of a postman with an empty sack makes him go doolally.

Mary Jameson: Born Edinburgh, 1914. Lived in Vietnam and member of the Communist Party of Great Britain.

Malcolm Lobban: retired civil servant from Vale of Leven. Editor of quarterly journal of Clan MacLennan Assoc. Writes articles on Scottish history. Nae-nonsense Scot.

Kevin MacNeil: born and raised on Isle of Lewis, educated at Nicolson Institute, University of Edinburgh, and Sabhal Mor Ostaig. Widely published. Lives in Skye.

Thom Nairn: Widely published, editor of *Cencrastus* magazine. Currently writing two works, *Sky Burial* and *Animal Heads.*

Eveline Pye: Born Glasgow. Had 10 years in Zambia working in Copper Mines. Single parent, lectures in Statistics at Glasgow Caledonian University. Amazed to find herself writing and performing poetry.

Stanley Robertson: Born 1940 into musical travelling family. Foremost Scottish storyteller and tradition-bearer, inheritor of song, ballad and story. Also writes Scottish Doric prose.

William Sharpton: has MSc. degree from University of Edinburgh. Currently independantly researching modern Scottish and Irish Literature. Also active musician, poet and free-lance journalist. Resides in Edinburgh and Boston, Massachusetts.

Henry Skwar (originally Skwarczynski): born in Poland, lives in Chicago with his wife Egle. The published story is part of collection *The Thirteenth Flemish Proverb.*

Raymond Soltysek: Born Barrhead, 1958. Has been writing for four years, with work included in *Rebel Inc.* and 1996 Harper Collins anthology. Now working on one man show of his short stories, with which hopes to "tour" in the near future.

Margaret Tait: Film maker. Writer/director of film *Blue Black Permanent.* Numerous short films, short stories and poetry.

Valerie Thornton: writes poems and short stories, and tutors creative writing workshops. Recently published educational textbook on creative writing, *Working Words.*

Phillip Whidden: books include a volume of poetry, *Fall from Decadence.* Other poems, articles and short stories have appeared in *The Edinburgh Review, Chapman, Spectrum, Insight* and other journals.

Kevin Williamson: a writer who dabbles in publishing. Born in the sixties. Grew up in north of Scotland. Lives in Edinburgh.